NEIL T. ANDERSON
& RICH MILLER

MANAGING
YOUR
ANGER

D1637361

HARVEST HOUSE PUBLISHERS
EUGENE, OREGON

Cover by Jason Gabbert Design

Cover photos © Shawn Hempel / shutterstock

MANAGING YOUR ANGER

Copyright © 2018 Neil T. Anderson/Rich Miller
Published by Harvest House Publishers
Eugene, Oregon 97408
www.harvesthousepublishers.com

ISBN 978-0-7369-5825-7 (pbk.)
ISBN 978-0-7369-7221-5 (eBook)

Library of Congress Cataloging-in-Publication Data

Names: Anderson, Neil T., 1942 – author. | Miller, Rich, 1954 – author.
Title: Managing your anger : experience restored relationships, complete
    forgiveness, and peace of mind / Neil T. Anderson, Rich Miller.
Other titles: Getting anger under control
Description: Eugene, Oregon : Harvest House Publishers, 2018. | Revised
    edition of: Getting anger under control / Neil T. Anderson and Rich
    Miller. copyright 2002.
Identifiers: LCCN 2017023233 (print) | LCCN 2017032841 (ebook) |
    ISBN 9780736972215 (ebook) | ISBN 9780736958257 (pbk.)
Subjects: LCSH: Anger—Religious aspects—Christianity.
Classification: LCC BV4627.A5 (ebook) | LCC BV4627.A5 A53 2018 (print) | DDC
    248.4—dc23
LC record available at https://lccn.loc.gov/2017023233

Printed in the United States of America

18 19 20 21 22 23 24 25 26 / BP-CD / 10 9 8 7 6 5 4 3 2

CONTENTS

INTRODUCTION

●

A vast majority of Americans feel their country has reached an ill-mannered watershed. Nine out of ten Americans think incivility is a serious problem, and nearly half think it is extremely serious. Seventy-eight percent say the problem has worsened in the last ten years."[1] That poll was taken twenty years ago when the global economy was relatively stable, 9/11 hadn't happened, ISIS was an unknown, and smart phones were in their infancy. How are we doing twenty years later? "Rage is today's ruling online emotion," so concluded a 2013 study of Chinese mini-blogging network Weibo—a platform that resembles Twitter and boasts twice as many users. Beihang University researchers examined 70 million Weibo "tweets" over a six-month period, sorting them by anger, joy, sadness, and disgust. Rage was the emotion most likely to spread across social media, with one angry post powerful and persuasive enough to negatively influence a follower of a follower of a follower.[2]

"We the people are ticked off. The body politic is burning up. And the anger that courses through our headlines and news feeds—about injustice and inequality, about marginalization and disenfranchisement, about what they are doing to us—shows no sign of abating…Half of all Americans are angrier today than they were a year ago."[3] That article was published in January 2016, before

Hillary Clinton and Donald Trump were nominated to represent their respective political parties. The presidential debates that followed reached an all-time low in civility. Thanks to the Internet, the world had front-row seats to witness the embarrassing charade. Many Americans were fuming with anger at one candidate or the other, and their only outlet was to wait until election day and cast one vote against the candidate they least liked. It is unlikely that a singular act of voting would be enough to put away all anger (see Ephesians 4:31). Protests erupted immediately after Donald Trump was voted to be the president of the United States.

Unjustified anger has scarred the landscape of humanity ever since Adam ate the forbidden fruit. Anger that rips apart homes, businesses, and countries is not new. The media-driven escalation of anger is unprecedented. Our smart phones notify us immediately with every terror attack, school shooting, political scandal, race riot, police shooting, and anonymous tips from every Tom, Sally, and Joe, who are not even authorized to speak of such things. Uncensored airways are fueling the fires of rage, and tech-savvy children can view every rant on their smart phones. One mother wrote to us:

> While you are at it, you might want to think about writing a book for angry teenagers. My 16-year-old daughter's anger has over the years slowly turned her mind away from Christ and toward the pop culture. Her situation is an ironic one that exists, I believe, in many homes where Christian school, church, and family values have been predominant. For her, the situation posed a dilemma. If she chose Christ, she would never "fit in." If she chose pop culture, she jeopardized her relationships at home and with this "distant" God who "doesn't care anyway, because He doesn't give me what I want." So she got stuck in angry defiance. At home, she acts out

her anger. At school, she's decided to get rougher and tougher so that she won't be hurt.

Looking back, I see that I was clueless about the roots of anger and the consequences of wrong thinking. On the outside, it seemed like we were on top of the situation. Yet there were critical stages of anger that we didn't have the tools to see or confront. Now we are doing major parental intervention in her life. Hopefully, it isn't too late.

With the world spiraling into chaos, why doesn't God do something? Jonah was asking the same question 2800 years ago. Nineveh, the capital of Assyria, was sliding into a crevasse of immorality and cruel violence. Jonah was angry at the people for not repenting and angry at God for not bringing judgment upon them. He wanted God to destroy Nineveh. Unlike Jonah, God is "slow to anger and abundant in lovingkindness, and one who relents concerning calamity" (Jonah 4:2). The Lord zeroed in on the critical issue when He asked Jonah a question we need to ask ourselves: "Do you have good reason to be angry?" (4:4).

Suppose we are in the "difficult," "terrible" (NIV), or "perilous" (KJV) end times that Paul said would come (2 Timothy 3:1). A time when "people will be lovers of themselves, lovers of money, boastful, proud, abusive, disobedient to parents, ungrateful, unholy, without love, unforgiving, slanderous, without self-control, brutal, not lovers of good, treacherous, rash, conceited, lovers of pleasure rather than lovers of God" (2 Timothy 3:2-4 NIV). Should we be angry like Jonah? Should we pray for God's judgment to come, or should we be like the Lord "not wishing for any to perish but for all to come to repentance" (2 Peter 3:9)? "What sort of people ought you to be in holy conduct and godliness, looking for and hastening the coming of the day of God, because of which the heavens will be destroyed by burning, and the elements will melt with intense heat!" (2 Peter 3:11). Paul's description of end-time culture seems a lot like the world we are living in, but it doesn't have to describe you. God has already staged His intervention. He has done all He needs to do for us to repent. It is up to us to put aside all anger. Our responsibility is to follow Paul's instruction in Ephesians 4:25-27, 29-32:

> Laying aside falsehood, speak truth to each one of you with his neighbor, for we are members of one another. Be angry, and yet do not sin; do not let the sun go down on your anger, and do not give the devil an opportunity...Let no unwholesome word proceed from your mouth, but only such a word as is good for edification according to the need of the moment, so that it will give grace to those who hear. Do not grieve the Holy Spirt of God, by whom you were sealed for the day of redemption. Let all bitterness and wrath and anger and clamor and slander be put away from you, along with all malice. Be kind to one another, tenderhearted, forgiving each other, just as God in Christ also has forgiven you.

Every evening the sun will set on the unresolved anger of millions of people. The devil takes advantage of the opportunity, and the Holy Spirit is grieved. Anger will never completely disappear from our lives this side of heaven. Nor should it. There is a time and place for anger under control. Righteous indignation is a God-ordained stimulus for righting that which is wrong, but unjustified anger is the master of the defeated. If we desire to be angry and not sin, then we need to be like Jesus, and be angry at sin. In this book we want to expose the roots of anger, and share how we can put away all "wrath and anger and clamor and slander" (Ephesians 4:31).

Following the order in the above passage (Ephesians 4:25-27), we will be explaining three different categories of anger, which require three different strategies for resolution. Paul first addresses anger that arises from everyday circumstances. In the course of any day, something will happen that just ticks us off. This can be a combination of our own immaturity, worldview, and how well our faith is grounded in reality. The end of the passage deals with anger issues that have origins in the past.

The second category has to do with old flesh patterns or mental strongholds and defense mechanisms. Every believer has a choice every moment to live by the Spirit or walk by the flesh. "The fruit of the Spirit is love, joy, peace, patience, kindness, goodness, faithfulness, gentleness, self-control" (Galatians 5:22-23). The word *patience* or *longsuffering* in Greek is *makrothumeo*, which is a conjunction of two words—*makros* meaning long and *thumos* meaning temper. The idea is "slow to anger" or a long time under duress before one gets angry. We shall see how critical the idea of control, or the lack thereof, relates to anger.

The deeds of the flesh include enmity, strife, outbursts of anger, rivalries, dissensions, and the like (Galatians 5:19-21). It is important to note that an "outburst of anger" is just one of many flesh patterns. It is our responsibility to overcome the flesh (5:24), not just one manifestation of it. The world is in its present shape because of the original sin that separated us from God. There is only one answer to the problem of sin and that is to be reconciled to God through genuine repentance and faith in Him. The tool we use to accomplish that is the *Steps to Freedom in Christ* (Steps), which are being used all over the world to resolve personal and spiritual conflicts. We have to get beyond "anger management," which is a means of keeping anger from erupting and doing harm to self and others, to remove the barriers between ourselves and God allowing the life of Christ to work through us. Then we can have peace, patience, and self-control, and

God is glorified in our bodies. The fruit of the Spirit is a manifestation of God's presence within us.

The third category has to do with healing the wounds of the past and setting captives free, which is what Jesus came to do. Wounds that are not transformed are transferred to others. Homes, work places, and churches are full of wounded people who bounce off one another's wounds. There is a major difference between people who get angry and angry people. Some are like caged animals who are ready to pounce the moment someone touches their sore spot.

Finally, our goal is to present a complete answer to the issue of anger. The apostle Paul wrote, "The Spirit clearly says that in later times some will abandon the faith and follow deceiving spirits and things taught by demons" (1 Timothy 4:1 NIV). We can tell you from personal experience (as can all of our staff), that this is presently happening all over the world. We have helped thousands of people who are struggling with blasphemous, condemning, and deceiving thoughts that have proven to be a spiritual battle for their minds. By processing the Steps they were able to get rid of those thoughts and experience a peaceful mind. Whether you agree or disagree with that analysis doesn't change the fact that "our struggle is not against flesh and blood, but against rulers, against authorities, against the powers of this dark world and against the spiritual forces of evil in the heavenly realms" (Ephesians 6:12 NIV).

One of each of the seven steps are listed at the end of chapters 2 through 8, and each begins with a prayer asking God to grant you repentance leading to a knowledge of the truth that will set you free (see 2 Timothy 2:24-26). We have also included discussion questions at the end of each chapter for group discussion. We believe that God is the Wonderful Counselor and the only One who can set you free. If you are processing this book in a group be assured that nobody needs to be embarrassed, and public disclosure is not required of anyone. The Steps are an encounter with God, not each other. If you are leading a group study on this book, see the appendix on page 213 for some guidelines.

Please, for your sake, don't just read the book; do the book. If you are dependent upon God, willing to repent, and believe the gospel you will be able to put off all bitterness, wrath, anger, clamor, and slander along with all malice. To illustrate why we believe that anger may just be the tip of the iceberg, read the following unsolicited testimony we received. They not only gave permission for us to share it, but encouraged us to do so that others may take similar steps.

> I am sure that you get many letters from people, but I felt I needed to share our story with you. I also know that you have heard many sordid things in your years in ministry so I will not hold back. Forgive me if I get too personal but I think you need to know it all to understand the magnitude of what has taken place. My boyfriend and I met a little over a year ago. We were both in relationships and found each other online in the "looking for an affair" section. We started having an affair and as we got to know each other better, we discovered that we had a lot in common.
>
> This was not a good thing. You see, both of us came from dysfunctional families with unhealthy religious backgrounds. He was raised in a Jehovah Witness "church" in which he was molested by several men and women of the congregation, including his mother and sister, beginning at age six. Sex (deviant sex) was love to him, so he lived his life in search of it. He is a sex addict. I grew up in a dysfunctional home and attended a very legalistic church. As a result of the neglect/abuse I suffered as a child, I learned that sex and men would give me what I was lacking. I too am a sex addict. There are many stories and dark experiences we both have had as a

result of this. There have been same sex encounters, multiple partners/affairs and involvement in sexually deviant behaviors too numerous to list. I cringe now when I think of what we both have seen and done, as individuals and as a couple.

Now add the rage disorder we both struggle with, the substance abuse issues, illegal activities and pretty much every other bondage you can think of. We were a couple of train wrecks. Since we got along so well, we decided to leave our marriages for each other, destroying families in the process. So here we are, living our lives doing anything and everything our flesh desired. Then one day we had a conversation about church. We both had come from religious backgrounds after all. It started out with a random thought but then something changed. We both had a desire to go back to church. We found one we both liked, but the guilt and shame we felt from our lives made it difficult. I wanted to run every time the worship started. I got very uneasy and antsy. I heard voices saying that I didn't belong. I wasn't like these other people. I was filth. My being there would only make them dirty instead of making me clean. I would have negative, and even evil thoughts toward the other people there. It was so unlike me. It went this way for a while.

I would go but I would shut down mentally as we entered the church so I got nothing out of it. Then one day I remembered the *Steps to Freedom in Christ*. I had taken the classes years prior in church, but never actually did the steps. I figured attending the class was close enough. Anyway, I ordered *Victory Over the Darkness* and *The Bondage Breaker*, but *The Bondage Breaker* came first so we started that. We were both having a hard time at first, but it was a little harder for me.

The day I KNEW Satan had hold of me was when my husband was trying to love me through one of the steps and a voice, not my own, told me to hurt him. I could feel my jaw clench and my eyes narrow as the hate rose up in me. I had a literal burning desire to harm him! The awareness in that moment that it was no longer me but Satan controlling me was indescribable, and it scared me straight. Since that day we both have surrendered to God.

We completed the *Steps to Freedom in Christ*. ALL of them! We are attending church every week, have daily devotions both together and privately. We pray and read the Word. We have stopped all of the sinful behaviors we were involved in before. Our anger has subsided. People have actually commented on the changes!

We have inner peace and the noise in my head is finally gone! We have become involved in ministry and are working diligently every day to serve our Lord in obedience. We have a real passion for people like us now and want to help others find the freedom we have found. The changes that have happened in our lives are nothing short of an act of God. Where we came from and where we are now makes me want to weep with gratitude, and I often do! The Lord is good and faithful and He never leaves us nor forsakes us…EVEN people like us! He was waiting with open arms!

CHAPTER ONE

ANGER AND PHYSICAL HEALTH

●

Anger: an acid that can do more harm to the vessel in which it is stored than to anything on which it is poured.

Attributed to Lucius Annaeus Seneca

Jim was trying to wrap up another busy day at the office. His son was having a Little League game at 5:30 and he promised him he would be there. Demands at work prevented him from being at the last three games. Jim was a highly motivated insurance salesman who had won the salesperson of the year award for three straight years. His desire to climb the corporate ladder was often in conflict with his Christian convictions to be a good husband and father, but it wasn't hard to rationalize his work ethic. Achievement awards, higher salaries, and greater commissions afforded him and his family a higher standard of living and better vacations.

Last minute calls irritated him as he rushed to get out the door. *Why do people always call at the last minute?* Jim wondered. He glanced at his watch as he merged into the late afternoon traffic. Just enough time to make it to the game on time if the freeways cooperate. As he tried to work his way into the fast lane, he was suddenly cut off by another car. *Stupid jerk! Where are the cops when you need them?* The traffic slowed to a crawl and Jim found himself stuck behind a large truck that blocked his view and slowed his lane even more. His hands gripped the steering wheel, and he angrily shouted, "Trucks shouldn't be allowed to drive anywhere other than the right lane!"

Ruminating thoughts in Jim's left cerebral cortex already sent a signal deeper in the brain to hypothalamic nerve cells. The activated hypothalamic emergency system stimulated sympathetic nerves to constrict the arteries carrying blood to Jim's skin, kidneys, and intestines. At the same time, the brain sent a signal to the adrenal glands, and they pumped large doses of adrenaline and cortisol into his bloodstream. As he sat behind the truck, his muscles tightened, his heart beat faster, and his blood pressure rose. In such a state his blood would clot more rapidly in case of injury. Muscles at the outlet of his stomach were squeezing down so tightly that nothing could leave his digestive tract causing it to become spastic, resulting in abdominal pain. The blood was directed away from the skin, making it feel cool and clammy, and toward the muscles to facilitate a "fight or flight" response.

As the angry thoughts continued, Jim's increased heart rate had pumped far more blood than was needed to just sit in the car. His body was prepared to spring into action, but there was nowhere to go. He was tempted to let off some steam by rolling down the window and telling somebody what he thought of them or honk the horn, but he knew that wouldn't do any good. The adrenaline stimulated Jim's fat cells to empty their content into the blood stream. This would provide additional energy that would be necessary if the situation required immediate action. But Jim just sat there, fuming at the traffic while his liver converted the fat into cholesterol. He has no one to fight and nowhere to take flight.

Over time the cholesterol formed from the unused fat in the bloodstream will accumulate. It morphs into a plaque in the arteries that begins to block the flow of blood. Jim's struggle with anger continues until one day the flow of blood is cut off entirely and Jim becomes one of the 500,000 Americans each year who suffer from a heart attack.

Tragically, some do take action when their anger gets the best of them. Their cars become weapons, or they find weapons to use against those who they think have caused them to get angry. More than 1000 people in the U.S. die each year in road rage incidents. U.S. academic James Strickland reported that if provoked, motorists would respond as follows:

- 40 percent driving more aggressively
- 22 percent make angry expressions
- 15 percent mutter under breath
- 14 percent hit something in the car
- 5 percent make obscene gestures
- 3 percent bump the car causing the anger
- Only 1 in 140 said they'd do nothing[1]

Oh no you're not! I'll speed up just a little and not let him in.

Are you kidding me? I have waited through two traffic lights to get through the intersection and a stupid cement truck is ahead of the pack. He could have gone through the yellow light. That slug will keep five cars from making it through when the light changes.

Why is that bimbo tailgating me? Doesn't she know it's against the law? I think I will just keep going slower and slower until she gets the message.

Why is this person in the fast lane?

Get off your stupid cell phone you idiot. The light changed two seconds ago.

Why are you shaking your fist at me? I'm trying to set a good example by driving under the speed limit.

I would love to give you a piece of my mind, but an icy stare will have to do as I drive by.

Listen to yourself! For the next week take special note of what you are thinking when you drive in traffic. To give another a piece of your mind is to rob your mind of peace, because anyone who shovels dirt at another is losing ground.

Too many people are at the boiling point, and the slightest provocation can set them off. "The famous psychologist, John Hunter, knew what anger could do to his heart: 'The first scoundrel that gets me angry will kill me.' Sometime later, at a medical meeting, a speaker made assertions that incensed Hunter. As he stood up and bitterly attacked the speaker, his anger caused such a contraction of blood vessels in his heart that he fell dead."[2]

Frederick Buechner wrote:

> Of the seven deadly sins, anger is possibly the most fun. To lick your wounds, to smack your lips over grievances long past, to roll over your tongue the prospect of bitter confrontations still to come, to savor to the last toothsome morsel both the pain you are given and the pain you are giving back; in many ways it is a feast fit for a king. The chief drawback is that what you are wolfing down is yourself. The skeleton at the feast is you.[3]

In my first pastorate, I (Neil) was given a book by an ambitious engineer in our church. He said, "You should read this book, because I think you may benefit from it." The book was *Type A Behavior and Your Heart* by Meyer Friedman and Ray Rosenman.[4] This highly motivated IBM engineer went on to explain that he had a Type A personality and he suspected that I did too. After reading the book, I did see some aspects of my personality that were Type A. I also gave a message a few weeks later entitled, "Jesus was Type B."

Friedman and Rosenman were cardiologists who began to notice that certain personality types were more prone to have heart problems. Those who burnt the candle at both ends, climbed the stairs two steps at a time, took little time off, and were driven to accomplish their goals were classified Type A. They are the task oriented, high achievers of this world, and they are driven to accomplish their goals. Type B individuals are more laid back, less driven, and generally more relational.

Their observations have had a profound effect on society. Not only are their classifications of Type A and B personalities well-known stereotypes, but they stimulated a flood of research into psychosomatic illnesses. Before the publication of their work, stress was not considered to be a major contributor to heart disease, cancer, and other major illnesses, but it is today. The medical field is now telling us that the majority of people are sick for psychosomatic reasons.

Redford and Virginia Williams, in their book *Anger Kills,*[5] adapted the work of Friedman and Rosenman to the problem of anger. In their research, they show how those with a hostile personality are more prone to coronary heart disease. For many years, researchers, therapists, and schools of higher education have used the MMPI (Minnesota Multiphasic Personality Inventory) to assess clients and students. Since many of these test results have been kept, they could be compared many years later with the physical health of those who took the test. The Williamses, along with other colleagues, isolated certain questions from the MMPI that reflected a cynical distrust of others, the frequent experience of angry feelings, and the overt expression of their cynicism in aggressive behavior. They summarize their findings as follows:

1. Hostile people—those with high levels of cynicism, anger and aggression—are at higher risk of developing

life-threatening illnesses than are their less hostile
counterparts.

2. By driving others away, or by not perceiving the support
   they could be deriving from their social contacts, hostile
   people may be depriving themselves of the health-
   enhancing, stress buffering benefits of social support.

3. A quicker activation of their flight-or-fight response, in
   combination with their relatively weak parasympathetic
   calming response, is a biologic mechanism that probably
   contributes to the health problems that afflict hostile
   people.

4. Hostile people also are more prone to engage in a
   number of risky behaviors—eating more, drinking more
   alcohol, smoking—that could damage their health.[6]

The fact that many people are sick for psychosomatic reasons
indicates that more is going on than just a biological response to the
environment. To understand how the body and soul interact, consider the following diagram:

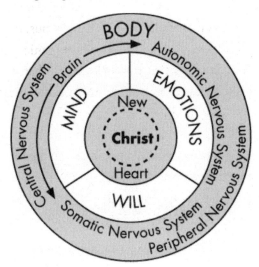

God formed Adam and Eve from the dust of the earth and breathed into them the breath of life (see Genesis 2:7). This union of divine breath and earthly dust is what constituted the physical and spiritual life that Adam and Eve both possessed. To be physically alive means that our soul is in union with our body. To be spiritually alive means that our soul (depicted as mind, emotion, and will in the diagram) is in union with God. When Adam and Eve sinned they were separated from God. They died spiritually. Physical death would also be a consequence of the fall, but that would happen years later.

Every human being possesses an inner person and an outer person. In other words we all have a material self and an immaterial self (see 2 Corinthians 4:16). Our outer person, or material part, is what makes up our physical body. We relate to the world around us through our five senses. The inner person or immaterial self describes the spirit and soul of a human being.[7] Being created in the image of God is why we have the capacity to think, feel, and choose, as opposed to animals that operate out of divine instinct.

Being fearfully and wonderfully made, it would only make sense that God would create the outer person to correlate with the inner person. The brain and mind correlation is obvious, but the two are fundamentally different. Our brains are like organic computers that will return to dust when we physically die. At that time, if we are born-again believers, we will be present with the Lord, but we will not be there mindlessly. The mind is part of the soul, the inner person.

The brain is the capstone of the central nervous system, which also includes the spinal cord. Using the computer analogy, if the brain is the hardware, then the mind is the software. As we shall explain later, the brain cannot function in any way other than how it has been programmed. Neither the software nor the hardware is any good without the other.

Branching off from the central nervous system is a peripheral nervous system that has two distinct channels. One channel is the somatic nervous system. That system regulates all our muscular and skeletal movements. It is that which we have volitional control over. Provided we have adequate physical health, we can mentally choose to move our limbs, smile, and speak. Obviously, the somatic nervous system correlates with our will. We don't do anything without first thinking it. The thought-action response may be so rapid that one is hardly aware of the sequence, but it is always there. Involuntary muscular movements do occur when the system breaks down, as is the case with Parkinson's disease.

The autonomic nervous system is that which regulates all our glands and correlates with our emotions. We don't have direct volitional control over the functioning of our glands. In the same way we don't have direct volitional control of our emotions including the feelings of anger. We cannot will ourselves to like someone who is disgusting. We can choose to do the loving thing on their behalf even though we don't like them. We cannot simply tell ourselves to stop being angry because we cannot directly manage our emotions that way. When we acknowledge that we are angry, we do have control over how we are going to express it. We can manage our behavior within limits, because that is something we have volitional control over. We do have control of what we will think and believe, and that is what controls what we do and how we feel.

Telling angry people that they shouldn't be angry will only produce guilt, defensiveness (rationalization), or retaliation. You will have as much success telling them to stop being angry as they will have trying to keep their autonomic nervous system from functioning. We can, however, be a calming influence so they can manage their behavior. "A gentle answer turns away wrath, but a harsh word stirs up anger" (Proverbs 15:1). We could say, "I know you are angry right now, and you may have good reason to be. Are you open to sharing with me what that reason is so I can understand?" Anger in others is a symptom that must be acknowledged, or you will be adding insult to injury.

It is important to realize that what is causing the autonomic nervous system to respond is not the brain, and neither is the brain causing us to feel angry. It is the mind and the way it has been programmed. Neither do the circumstances of life or other people make us angry. It is our perception of those people and events and how we interpret them and that is a function of our minds and how they have been programmed.

Let's apply that reasoning to the problem of stress. When the pressures of life begin to mount, our bodies try to adapt. Our adrenal glands will excrete hormones into our bloodstream enabling us to rise to the challenge. If the pressure persists too long, then stress becomes distress, our system breaks down, and we become sick. Why then do some people respond positively to stress while others get sick? Is it because one has superior adrenal glands? Some are physically able to handle more than others, but that is not the primary difference. The primary difference is found in the mind not the body.

Suppose two partners in a business are confronted with what one believes is a financial crisis. They just lost a contract they thought would bring them to a new level of prosperity. One partner is not a Christian and has chosen to believe that this new contract would make him successful. Many of his personal goals would be realized, but now his dreams are dashed. He responds in anger to all who try to console him and calls his lawyer to see if he can sue the company who broke the contract.

The other partner is a Christian who believes that success is becoming the person God created him to be. He believes that God will supply all his needs. Therefore, this loss has less of an impact on him. Though he will likely be disappointed, he doesn't get angry, because he sees this temporary setback at work as a learning experience and continues to believe that all things work together for good to those who trust God (Romans 8:28). One of these two partners is stressed out and angry while the other partner isn't. The primary difference between the two men is their belief system, not their external circumstances, which are the same. "For as he thinks within himself, so he is" (Proverbs 23:7).

This brings up another important concept. If what we believe does not conform to truth, then what we feel does not conform to reality. Suppose a man has been employed by the same company for 30 years. His plan is to work another five or ten years with the same company and then retire. The recent recession has resulted in some layoffs, but he believes his job is safe. Then on a Monday morning he receives an email from his boss requesting that he come to his office Friday morning at 10:00. Can you imagine what would go through his mind that week? *Why does he want to see me at the end of the week? They are going to lay me off!* If that is what he thinks he will likely get angry. *How can they lay me off after thirty years of service? I'm not going to give them the satisfaction. I'm going to resign!*

His wife talks him out of it, but on Tuesday and Wednesday he is struggling with doubts. *Well, maybe they aren't going to lay me off. Yeah they are. No they're not. Yeah they are!* Now he is feeling anxious, because he is double-minded. By Thursday he has convinced himself that he is probably going to get laid off. *How am I going to get a job at my age? How will I pay the bills?* Now he is depressed, because he feels helpless and hopeless. By Friday morning he is an emotional wreck. Reluctantly he enters the office of his boss who says, *Congratulations. We are promoting you to vice president.* In those five days he has felt anger, anxiety, and depression all as a result of what he has chosen to think. None of it was based in reality.

Current or external events do not trigger our physiological responses, nor is the secretion of adrenaline initiated by our adrenal glands. External events are picked up by our five senses and sent as a signal to our brains. The mind then interprets the data, choices are made, and that is what determines the signal that is sent from the central nervous system to the peripheral nervous system. The brain cannot function any other way than how it has been programmed.

If the data we receive is false or incomplete then wrong decisions are made and the emotional response is inappropriate. Many civil protests have turned into angry riots, destroying property and taking human lives. Often it is fueled by false or incomplete information supplied by agitators with their own agenda. Few people listen to reason when anger takes over. Some don't want to wait for justice to be served, because they don't trust the justice system.

Our emotions and actions reveal what we believe. People don't always live according to what they profess, but they do live according to what they believe. James wrote, "I will show you my faith by my works" (James 2:18).

Let's take another look at Jim, our angry driver. He held certain beliefs about himself, life, and what he valued. Chances are his identity and sense of worth were tied into his career. He believed he would be a successful person if he did well on the job and a failure if he didn't. He also had a belief about himself. He was a salesman and a good one. But he was also a father and he held certain Christian values about being a good parent. That afternoon he didn't want to go back on his word and miss his son's game, but he didn't want to miss a couple of late-afternoon calls either that could affect his sales. Was he a salesman first or a father first?

Jim made choices that afternoon that had a profound effect on how he felt. He could have entered into his phone the time of his son's game and made it just as important as any business schedule. Then he could have left earlier and avoided all the traffic. His secretary could simply tell his callers that he had an important commitment that he could not miss, but he will do his best to get back to them tomorrow. The stalled traffic didn't make him angry, that was his own emotional response to the choices he made that day.

When I attended my first doctoral class years ago, I was the only professing Christian enrolled. The instructor was an ex-nun who liked to show off her liberation from the church with a lot of profanity. I think she was especially delighted to have a "reverend" in her class whom she would often put on the spot. I saw it as a challenge to my faith, which I was delighted to accept. Near the end of the semester, we were asked to share with the class what our term paper would be. I said I was doing a paper on managing our anger. Another doctoral student protested, "You can't do a paper on managing your anger." I asked her, "Why not?" "Because you don't get angry." She thought it was incredulous that I would choose to do a paper on anger and she reminded me of it several times. I assured her that I do at times get angry.

Apparently, she would have responded in anger to some of the targeting that I was getting in the class. Our differences became clearer as the semester came to an end. She and her brother, who also attended the class, were members of a cult. Our divergent belief systems became more and more evident as they were tested under fire. What we believe does affect how we respond to the circumstances of life. If our identity and security are centered in our eternal relationship with God, then the temporal things of life have less of an impact on us.

No person can consistently behave in a way that isn't consistent with what they believe about themselves. What you do doesn't determine who you are. Who you are determines what you do. So who are you? "See what kind of love the Father has given to us, that we should be called children of God; and so we are" (1 John 3:1 ESV).

Beloved, this is who you are:

You Are Accepted

John 1:12	You are God's child.
John 15:15	You are Jesus's chosen friend.
Romans 5:1	You have been justified (forgiven) and have peace with God.
1 Corinthians 6:17	You are united with the Lord and one with Him in spirit.
1 Corinthians 6:20	You have been bought with a price—you belong to God.
1 Corinthians 12:27	You are a member of Christ's body, part of His family.
Ephesians 1:1	You are a saint.
Ephesians 1:5	You have been adopted as God's child.
Ephesians 2:18	You have direct access to God through the Holy Spirit.
Colossians 1:14	You have been bought back (redeemed) and forgiven of all your sins.
Colossians 2:10	You are complete in Christ.

You Are Secure

Romans 8:1-2	You are free from condemnation.
Romans 8:28	You are assured that all things work together for good.

Romans 8:31	You are free from any condemning charges against you.
Romans 8:35	You cannot be separated from the love of God.
2 Corinthians 1:21-22	You have been established, anointed, and sealed by God.
Colossians 3:3	You are hidden with Christ in God.
Philippians 1:6	You are assured that the good work that God has begun in you will be finished.
Philippians 3:20	You are a citizen of heaven.
2 Timothy 1:7	You have not been given a spirit of fear, but of power, love, and a sound mind.
Hebrews 4:16	You can find grace and mercy in time of need.
1 John 5:18	You are born of God and the evil one cannot touch you.

You Are Significant

Matthew 5:13-14	You are the salt and light of the world.
John 15:1,5	You are a part of the true vine, joined to Christ and able to produce much fruit.
John 15:16	You have been chosen by Jesus to bear fruit.
Acts 1:8	You are a personal witness of Christ's.
1 Corinthians 3:16	You are God's temple where the Holy Spirit dwells.
2 Corinthians 5:17-18	You are at peace with God and He has given you the work of making peace between Himself and other people. You are a minister of reconciliation.
2 Corinthians 6:1	You are God's co-worker.
Ephesians 2:6	You are seated with Christ in the heavenlies.

Ephesians 2:10   You are God's workmanship.

Ephesians 3:12   You may approach God with freedom and confidence.

Philippians 4:13   You can do all things through Christ who strengthens you.

Discussion Questions

1. Why do so many people get angry while driving?

2. What can drivers control and what can't they control?

3. What is the difference between the outer person and the inner person?

4. What is the difference between physical life and spiritual life?

5. How would you cure a psychosomatic illness?

6. Why shouldn't we try telling people not to feel a certain way?

7. What should we do or tell people when we feel their emotions don't reflect reality?

8. How does belief affect how we act and feel?

9. What are common stimuli that turn protests into angry riots?

10. Why is it so important to know who you are?

Introduction to the *Steps to Freedom in Christ*

God created Adam and Eve in His image and in His likeness. They were physically and spiritually alive, and the latter means that their souls were in union with God. Living in a dependent relationship with their Heavenly Father, they were to rule over the birds of the sky, the beasts of the field, and the fish of the sea. Adam and Eve were accepted, secure, and significant. Acting independently of God, they chose to disobey Him, and their choice to sin separated them from God (see Genesis 2:15–3:13). They immediately felt fearful, anxious, depressed, and insecure. Because Eve was deceived by Satan and because Adam sinned, all their descendants are born physically alive but spiritually dead (Ephesians 2:1).

Since all have sinned (Romans 3:23), those who remain separated from God will struggle with personal and spiritual conflicts. Satan became the rebel holder of authority and the god of this world. Jesus referred to him as the ruler of this world, and the apostle John wrote that the whole world lies in the power of the evil one (1 John 5:19).

Jesus came to undo the works of Satan (1 John 3:8) and take upon Himself the sins of the world. By dying for our sins, Jesus removed the barrier that existed between God and those He created in His image. The resurrection of Christ brought new life to those who put their trust in Him.

Every born-again believer's soul is again in union with God and that is most often communicated in the New Testament by saying "in Christ," or "in Him." The apostle Paul explained that anyone who is in Christ is a new creation (2 Corinthians 5:17). The apostle John wrote, "But as many as received Him, to them He gave the right to become children of God, even to those who believe in His name" (John 1:12), and he also wrote, "See how great a love the Father has bestowed on us, that we would be called children of God; and such we are" (1 John 3:1).

No amount of effort on your part can save you, and neither can any religious activity, no matter how well intentioned. We are saved by faith, by what we choose to believe. All that remains for us to do is to put our trust in the finished work of Christ. "For by grace you have been saved through faith; and that not of yourselves, it is a gift of God; not as a result of works, so that no one may boast" (Ephesians 2:8-9). If you have never received Christ, you can do so right now. God knows the thoughts and intentions of your heart, so all you have to do is put your trust in God alone.

You can express your decision in prayer as follows:

> *Dear Heavenly Father, thank You for sending Jesus to die on the cross for my sins. I acknowledge that I have sinned and that I cannot save myself. I believe that Jesus came to give me life, and by faith I now choose to receive You into my life as my Lord and Savior. May the power of Your indwelling presence enable me to be the person You created me to be. I pray that You would grant me repentance, leading to a knowledge of the truth so that I can experience my freedom in Christ and be transformed by the renewing of my mind. In Jesus's precious name I pray. Amen.*

Assurance of Salvation

Paul wrote, "If you confess with your mouth Jesus as Lord, and believe in your heart that God raised Him from the dead, you will be saved" (Romans 10:9). Do you believe that God the Father raised Jesus from the dead? Did you invite Jesus to be your Lord and Savior? Then you are a child of God and nothing can separate you from the love of Christ (Romans 8:35). "And this is the testimony, that God has given us eternal life, and this life is in His Son. He who has the Son has life; he who does not have the Son of God does not have the life" (1 John 5:11-13). Your Heavenly Father has sent His Holy Spirit to bear witness with your spirit that you are a child of God (Romans 8:16). "You were sealed *in Him* with the Holy Spirit of promise" (Ephesians 1:13, emphasis added). The Holy Spirit will guide you into all truth (John 16:13).

Resolving Personal and Spiritual Conflict

Since we are all born dead (spiritually) in our trespasses and sin (Ephesians 2:1), we had neither the presence of God in our lives nor the knowledge of His ways. Consequently, we all learned to live independently of God. When we became new creations in Christ, our minds were not instantly renewed. That is why Paul wrote, "Do not conform any longer to the pattern of this world, but be transformed by the renewing of your mind. Then you will be able to test and approve what God's will is—His good, pleasing and perfect will" (Romans 12:2 NIV). That is why new Christians struggle with many of the same old thoughts and habits. Their minds have been previously programmed to live independently of God, and that is the chief characteristic of our flesh. As new creations in Christ we have the mind of Christ, and the Holy Spirit will lead us into all truth.

To experience our freedom in Christ and grow in the grace of God requires repentance, which literally means a change of mind. God will enable that process as we submit to Him and resist the devil (James 4:7). The *Steps to Freedom in Christ* (Steps) are designed to help you do that. Submitting to God is the critical issue. He is the Wonderful Counselor and the One who grants repentance leading to a knowledge of the truth (2 Timothy 2:24-26). The Steps cover seven critical issues that affect our relationship with God. We will not experience our freedom in Christ if we seek false guidance, believe lies, fail to forgive others as we have been forgiven, live in rebellion, respond in pride, fail to acknowledge our sin, and continue in the sins of our ancestors. "He who conceals transgressions will not prosper, but he who confesses and forsakes [renounces] them will find compassion" (Proverbs 28:13). "Therefore since we have this ministry, as we received mercy, we do not lose heart, but we have renounced things hidden because of shame, not walking in craftiness or adulterating the word of God, but by the manifestation of truth" (2 Corinthians 4:1-2).

Even though Satan is defeated, he still rules this world through a hierarchy of demons who tempt, accuse, and deceive those who fail to put on the armor of God, stand firm in their faith, and take every thought captive to the obedience of Christ. Our sanctuary is our identity and position in Christ, and we have all the protection we need to live a victorious life, but if we fail to assume our responsibility and give ground to Satan, we will suffer the consequences of our sinful attitudes and actions. The good news is, we can repent and reclaim all that we have in Christ, and that is what the Steps will enable you to do.

Processing the Steps

The best way to go through the Steps is to process them with a trained encourager. The book *Discipleship Counseling* explains the theology and process. However, you can also go through the Steps on your own. Every Step is explained so you will have no trouble doing that. If you are in a group study, the leader will introduce each Step after the discussion questions and ask you to pray the beginning prayer out loud. The rest you will process on your own. If you experience some mental interference, just ignore it and continue on. Thoughts such as, *This isn't going to work*, or *I don't believe this*, or blasphemous, condemning, and accusing thoughts have no power over you unless you believe them. They are just thoughts and it doesn't make any difference if they originate from yourself, an external source, or from Satan and his demons.

Such thoughts have no power over you unless you believe them. They will be resolved when you have fully repented. The mind is the control center, and you will not lose control if you can maintain control of your mind. The best way to do that, if you are being mentally harassed, is to just share it. Exposing the lies to the light breaks their power.

The apostle Paul wrote that "Satan disguises himself as an angel of light" (2 Corinthians 11:14). It is not uncommon for some to have thoughts or hear voices that claim to be friendly, offer companionship, or claim to be from God. They may even say that Jesus is Lord, but they cannot say that Jesus is their Lord. If there is any doubt about their origin, verbally ask God to show you the true nature of such spirit guides. You don't want any spirit guide other than the Holy Spirit to guide you.

Remember, you are a child of God and seated with Christ in the heavenlies (spiritual realm). That means you have the authority and power to do His will. The Steps don't set you free. Jesus sets you free, and you will progressively experience that freedom as you respond to Him in faith and repentance. Don't worry about any demonic interference, most do not experience any. It doesn't make any difference if Satan has a little role or a bigger role, the critical issue is your relationship with God, and that is what you are resolving. This is a ministry of reconciliation. Once those issues are resolved, Satan has no right to remain. Successfully completing this repentance process is not an end, it is a beginning of growth. Unless these issues are resolved, however, the growth process will be stalled and your Christian life will be stagnant.

Breaking Mental Strongholds

On a separate piece of paper write down any false beliefs and lies that surface during the Steps, especially those that are not true about yourself and God. When you are finished, verbally say for each exposed falsehood: "I renounce the lie that" (what you have believed), and "I announce the truth that" (what you are now choosing to believe is true based on God's Word). It may be best to have the encourager keep this list for you if you are being led by another through the Steps. We strongly recommend that you repeat the process of renouncing lies and choosing truth for forty days since we are transformed by the renewing of our minds (Romans 12:2), and it is very easy to defer back to old flesh patterns when tempted.

Preparation

Processing these Steps will play a major role in your journey of becoming more and more like Jesus so that you can be a fruitful disciple. The purpose is to become firmly rooted in Christ. It doesn't take long to establish your identity and freedom in Christ, but there is no such thing as instant maturity. Renewing your mind and conforming to the image of God is a lifelong process. May God grace you with His presence as you seek to do His will. Once you have experienced your freedom in Christ you can help others experience the joy of their salvation. You are now ready to begin the Steps by saying the prayer and declaration below.

Prayer

> *Dear Heavenly Father, You are present in this room and in my life. You alone are all-knowing, all-powerful, and present everywhere, and I worship You alone. I declare my dependency upon You, for apart from You I can do nothing. I choose to believe Your Word, which teaches that all authority in heaven and on earth belongs to the resurrected Christ, and being alive in Christ I have the authority to resist the devil as I submit to You. I ask that You fill me with Your Holy Spirit and guide me into all truth. I ask for Your complete protection and guidance as I seek to know You and do Your will. In the wonderful name of Jesus I pray. Amen.*

Declaration

In the name and authority of the Lord Jesus Christ, I com-mand Satan and all evil spirits to release their hold on me in order that I can be free to know and choose to do the will of God. As a child of God who is seated with Christ in the heavenly places, I declare that every enemy of the Lord Jesus Christ in my presence be bound. God has not given me a spirit of fear, therefore I reject any and all condemning, accusing, blasphemous, and deceiving spirits of fear. Satan and all his demons cannot inflict any pain or in any way prevent God's will from being done in my life today, because I belong to the Lord Jesus Christ.

CHAPTER TWO

ANGER AND MENTAL HEALTH

●

It is the intermittent fever which bespeaks unintermittent disease within; the occasional bubble escaping to the surface which betrays some rottenness underneath; a sample of the most hidden products of the soul dropped involuntarily when off one's guard; in a word, the lightening form of a hundred hideous and unchristian sins. For a want of patience, a want of kindness, a want of generosity, a want of courtesy, a want of unselfishness, are all instantaneously symbolized in one flash of temper. Hence it is not enough to deal with temper. We must go to the source, and change the inmost nature...by putting something in—a great love, a new Spirit, the Spirit of Christ...This only can eradicate what is wrong, work a chemical change, renovate...the inner man.[1]

Henry Drummond, *The Greatest Thing in the World*

It was the first evening of the conference and I couldn't help but notice a young lady sitting in the front row glaring at me. Her anger couldn't be disguised, and it seemed directed at me. After the session I was talking with some attendees when the angry lady's friend approached me and asked, "Can you help my friend? She can't get out of her seat."

As I walked over to her, I sensed the spiritual nature of her problem. I encouraged her to just relax and sit there for a few more minutes, and then she would be able to get up. I turned to help some others, and she approached me about ten minutes later asking for an appointment. We met two days later. I led her through the Steps, and God set her free with no residue of anger. It turned out she was a psychiatric nurse. She had pursued that career hoping to find some answers for herself, but none of her training addressed the spiritual bondage she was in. At the end of the conference she handed me a large wrapped package with a note that read, "You washed my feet, let me wash yours." Inside was a plastic basin that would heat the water for one's feet along with a gentle massaging action.

Psychiatry approaches mental health from a natural biochemical perspective. We value their contribution and have great respect for the science of medicine. Neurological problems do exist, and we are grateful for the advancement of science that can cure or bring some relief to those who suffer. Taking a pill to cure your body is commendable, but taking a pill to cure your soul isn't. Christians and not-yet Christians observe the same symptoms in psychosomatic disorders but may draw different conclusions as to the origin of the problem. Good mental health is generally defined as being in touch with reality and relatively free of anxiety. Let's consider that definition from a Christian worldview, faith-based perspective. For believers, the ultimate reality is God. Apart from Him nothing exists. If you are in touch with reality, you are in touch with God.

Hidden Agenda

Paul wrote, "So we do not lose heart. Though our outer nature is wasting away, our inner nature is being renewed day by day. For this light momentary affliction is preparing for us an eternal weight of glory beyond all comparison, as we look not to the things that are seen but to the things that are unseen. For the things that are seen are transient, but the things that are unseen are eternal" (2 Corinthians 4:16-18 ESV). For 1500 years, Christians have been saying the

Nicene Creed that begins with, "I believe in one God, the Father Almighty, Maker of heaven and earth, and of all things visible and invisible." The invisible spiritual realm is just as real as the chair you are sitting on. We can't see the spiritual world via our natural senses, but we can see the effect. Just like you can't see the signal that is coming through the airways to your cell phone, but you can hear it ring. "We know that we are of God, and that the whole world lies in the power of the evil one" (1 John 5:19). Do we know that? Do we know that Satan is the father of lies and has deceived the whole world (Revelation 12:9)? If we are deceived, however, we don't know it.

Anybody victimized by the father of lies would be considered mentally ill by secular therapists. If someone were to share the blasphemous, accusing, tempting thoughts and voices that they are struggling with, the doctor would likely prescribe an antipsychotic medication to help them with their "chemical imbalance." That is the only option if one is unaware of the spiritual world. But how could a chemical of any kind produce a personality and a thought? How could our neurotransmitters randomly fire, producing a thought that we are opposed to thinking? There is no natural explanation for that, but what you may hear is, "the voices stopped or were muted after the medication." Sure, but the symptoms are only masked when narcotized. Remove the medicine and the oppressive thoughts are back, so nothing was resolved. The same thing happens when people drink excessively and take drugs. They have no mental peace so they drown out the noise in their heads with chemicals only to wake up the next morning a little worse off than they were the day before. Paul wrote, "I am afraid that as the serpent deceived Eve by his cunning, your thoughts [*noema*]² will be led astray from a sincere and pure devotion to Christ" (2 Corinthians 11:3 ESV).

The criteria of being relatively free of anxiety is valid. Of the twenty-five uses of the word *anxiety* in Scripture, five are positive. If your teenager is two hours late getting home at night you should sense a little anxiety if you care for the kid. If you have an important exam tomorrow, you will feel some anxiety and the proper response is to pray and prepare. Severe anxiety, however, is crippling. The Greek word for anxiety is *merimna*, which is a combination of *merizo* (divide) and *nous* (mind). Anyone paying attention to a deceiving spirit is going to be double-minded and therefore anxious. James wrote that a double-minded person is unstable in all their ways (1:8). Since our emotions are a product of our thoughts, you can see how important it is to take every thought captive to the obedience of Christ as the following testimony we received via email illustrates:

> For years I had these voices in my head. There were four in particular and sometimes what seemed like loud choruses of them. When the subject of schizophrenia would come up on the media I would think to myself, "I know I am not schizophrenic, but what is this in my head?" I was tortured, mocked, jeered, and every single thought I had was second guessed. Consequently, I had zero self-esteem. I often used to wish the voices would be quiet, and I always wondered if other people had this as well, and if it was "common."
>
> When I started to learn from you about taking every thought captive to the obedience of Christ, and read about other people's experiences with voices, I came to recognize them for what they were, and I was able to make them leave. That was an amazing and beautiful experience, to be fully quiet in my mind after so many years of torment.

A simple way to test the origin of your thoughts is to ask, "Where did that thought come from? Did it come from a loving God? Did

I consciously choose to think that thought? Did I want to think that thought?" If you have never understood that people can pay attention to deceiving spirits, then you are going to conclude that all those thoughts are yours, which will only lead to personal defeat, damaged emotions, and sinful behavior. You can't blame the devil for your anger, but if you haven't "fastened on the belt of truth" (Ephesians 6:14 ESV), and taken "up the shield of faith, with which you can extinguish all the flaming darts of the evil one" (6:16 ESV), you may find yourself in bondage to his lies. Even if you have, there is good news. You can resolve that and have peace of mind if you repent by submitting to God and resisting the devil (James 4:7), which is what the Steps are designed to do.

Research Results

There have been several exploratory studies that have shown the effectiveness of the *Steps to Freedom in Christ*. Judith King, a Christian therapist, did several pilot studies. All three of these studies were performed on participants who attended a Living Free in Christ conference and were led through the Steps at the conclusion of the conference.

The first study involved 30 participants, who took a ten-item questionnaire before completing the Steps. The questionnaire was readministered three months after their participation. The questionnaire assessed for levels of depression, anxiety, inner conflict, tormenting thoughts, and addictive behaviors. The second study involved 55 participants, who took a 12-item questionnaire before completing the Steps that was then readministered three months later. The third pilot study involved 21 participants, who also took a 12-item questionnaire before receiving the Steps and then again three months afterward. The following table illustrates the *percentage of improvement* for each category.

	Depression	Anxiety	Inner Conflict	Tormenting Thoughts	Addictive Behavior
Pilot Study 1	64%	58%	63%	82%	52%
Pilot Study 2	47%	44%	51%	58%	43%
Pilot Study 3	52%	47%	48%	57%	39%

The Living Free in Christ conference is now available as a curriculum entitled *Freedom in Christ Discipleship Course*. The curriculum includes a leader's guide with the messages written out, a learner's guide for each participant, which includes The Steps to Freedom, and a DVD with lessons taught by the staff of Freedom in Christ Ministries.

The Board of the Ministry of Healing[3] based in Tyler, Texas, conducted more thorough research using psychologically normed scales. The study completed at Tyler, Texas, took place in cooperation with a doctoral student at Regent University under the supervision of Dr. Fernando Garzon (Doctor of Psychology). Most people attending a Living Free in Christ conference or *Freedom in Christ Discipleship Course* can work through the repentance process on their own using the Steps. In our experience, about 15 percent can't because of severe life difficulties they have experienced. Those who can't work through the process themselves are offered a personal session with a trained lay encourager. These participants from our Oklahoma City, OK, and Tyler, TX, conferences were given a pretest before their Steps session with a lay encourager and a post-test three months later with the following results given in *percentage of improvement*:

	Oklahoma City, OK	Tyler, TX
Depression	44%	52%
Anxiety	45%	44%
Fear	48%	49%
Anger	36%	55%
Tormenting Thoughts	51%	27%
Negative Habits	48%	43%
Sense of Self-Worth	52%	40%

We believe that mental health begins with a true knowledge of God and a true knowledge of who we are in Christ. If you are a child of God, connected to Him in a liberating way, know that your sins are forgiven, that He will meet all your needs, that He will never leave you or forsake you, that He has gone before you to prepare a place for you for all eternity, that He loves you unconditionally, that the peace of God will guard your heart and your mind in Christ Jesus, would you be mentally healthy? Of course you would, unless you really do have a neurological problem.

On the other hand, mental illness is a distorted concept of God and of self. If you don't think that is true then visit a mental hospital and you will find some very religious people, but their view of God and of themselves is distorted. The secular staff have observed this and conclude that religion is part of their problem and not the answer. Religious fanaticism is a global problem, but a righteous relationship with God is our only hope. The apostle Paul would conclude that both secular practitioners and clients "are darkened in their understanding, alienated from the life of God because of the ignorance that is in them, due to their hardness of heart" (Ephesians 4:18 ESV).

Early Warning System

One might be tempted to think that it would be good to never be angry, anxious or depressed, but that is not true. Emotions are a vital part of our human existence. We were created to laugh and cry, to feel and care. We should long for emotional freedom, but we need to be set free from emotional bondage. It is often said that we can't trust our feelings, and there is some truth in that, but it is never right to deny them.

Emotions are an early warning system like an indicator light on the dash of your car. Suppose you are driving at night when a bright warning light comes on. There are three ways you can respond. First, since the light is a little irritating you can cover it up. That is called *suppression*. Second, you can get rid of the light by smashing it. That is *indiscriminant expression*. Third, you can look under the hood. That is *acknowledgment*.

Suppression is a conscious denial of what we are thinking and feeling. According to Dr. J.R. Averill, 90 percent of people stuff their anger inside while responding outwardly in a passive, submissive manner.[4] This "silent majority" actually harbors the most anger but does little about it.[5]

There are two major problems with suppressing our anger. First, it is dishonest. Communication between two people is about 8 percent verbal, about 37 percent behavioral, and 55 percent attitudinal. In other words there is verbal and nonverbal communication. When verbal and nonverbal don't match, which do you believe? In most cases people believe the nonverbal. That doesn't mean the verbal isn't important. In fact it is critically important, which is why Paul wrote, "Therefore, having put aside falsehood, let each one of you speak the truth with his neighbor, for we are members of one another. Be angry and do not sin; do not let the sun go down on your anger, and give no opportunity [literally; a place] to the devil" (Ephesians 4:25-27 ESV).

Second, suppression is unhealthy. David wrote, "Blessed is the man against whom the LORD counts no iniquity, and in whose spirit there is no deceit. For when I kept silent, my bones wasted away through my groaning all day long" (Psalm 32:2-3 ESV). Such is the nature of psychosomatic illnesses.

Repressed memories are an unconscious denial of past events, which are usually traumatic experiences that can affect people all their lives unless they are recovered and dealt with. Past physical wounds would have likely healed. It is the emotional wounds that are keeping people in bondage to the past. They are not in bondage to past traumas. They are in bondage to the lies they have believed as a result of the trauma, such as, *I'm no good. God doesn't love me. I'm worthless. Nobody cares for me. I'll never amount to anything.* Such deeply embedded lies leave victims feeling anxious and depressed. Some are filled with rage and don't know why. Secular therapists are aware of this and employ various techniques to discover what those past traumas are. We have found it far more fruitful to ask God to reveal to our minds painful memories and the lies behind them.[6] They often surface when people process the Steps.

Most believers want to live a responsible and manageable life, but they can only process what they know. The apostle Paul comments in 1 Corinthians 4:2-5 on the relative value of judging ourselves and receiving the judgment of others:

> Moreover, it is required of stewards that one be found trustworthy. But with me it is a very small thing that I should be examined by you or by any human court; in fact, I do not even examine myself. For I am conscious of nothing against myself, yet I am not by this acquitted;

but the one who examines me is the Lord. Therefore do not go on passing judgment before the time, but wait until the Lord comes who will both bring to light the things hidden in darkness and disclose the motives of men's hearts; and then each man's praise will come to him from God.

We agree with Leon Morris that judgment in this passage "does not denote the passing of final judgment, but the process of critical examination."[7] That is to scrutinize self and others. We could be like Paul and say, "I have dealt with my issues and sense no further conviction from God. That doesn't mean that I am perfect, it just means that I am not aware of my own imperfections, which God will reveal in His timing. I am not going to involve myself in some morbid introspection, and I am not going to let you scrutinize me either." If there are some dark moments in your past, God will reveal that to you in His timing. We have told hundreds of people, "Stop trying to figure out what is wrong with you when God hasn't revealed anything. Find out what is true about being a new creation in Christ. That is your ticket to being set free from your past." The surer you are of the answer to what a new creation in Christ is all about, the more able and willing you will be to deal with the problem. If you couldn't handle the trauma at the time, what makes you think you can now if you haven't matured in Christ? When we show ourselves faithful in little things, God will entrust us with bigger things.

Severely traumatized people often don't start recovering painful memories until later in life. In His graciousness God waits until they have enough maturity to deal with it, and even then He doesn't reveal everything all at once. It is like peeling layers off an onion. God starts with the outer layer, which is what you are conscious of. When that is dealt with He reveals the next layer of painful memories until they are all acknowledged and dealt with. I have seen some go through two or three layers in one conference, and I believe that happens because they are given an opportunity to resolve their personal and spiritual conflicts. We should never open a wound without having the means to close it.

The second alternative when we become aware of our emotional state is *indiscriminant expression.* "I just have to get this off my chest." *BLAP!* "There, I feel better." You may temporarily feel better after an outburst of anger, but chances are the other person doesn't, and you probably won't either when you regain your composure. Recall is inhibited, reason is thrown aside, and words are said that can't be taken back during outbursts of anger.

Third, the right response to emotional indicators is *acknowledgment,* to look under the hood. That is what the rest of this book is going to help you do, and we will start by showing the interconnection of faith and feeling.

Living by Faith

Faith is the operating principle of life. We are saved by faith, and we live by faith. Even the secular world lives by faith. The difference between Christian and non-Christian faith is the object of our faith. The question is not if you believe, but what or whom you believe. The goal for every believer is to know God and His ways and live accordingly by faith in the power of the Holy Spirit. The writer of Hebrews admonishes us to "run with endurance the race that is set before us, fixing our eyes on Jesus, the author and perfecter of our faith" (12:1-2). The problem is, we have not yet been perfected in our faith. We are not running the race in the right way if our faith is misguided, and that misguided faith will reveal itself by our actions and attitudes. You can't arrive at the right destination if you are on the wrong path.

Since our emotions are primarily a function of what we think, then it only stands to reason that anger, anxiety, and depression are revealing what we are thinking or believing. When we plan our days, we proceed by faith with the hope that our plans can be fulfilled. *I'll drop the kids off at school before I go to work.* That's a good plan, but how do you feel when you discover that the last person who drove the car used all the fuel and the car won't start? You have worked hard to get a promotion at work, but you are being passed over again, and a co-worker got the job. How would you feel? We get angry when our plans are blocked, anxious when they are uncertain, and depressed when they seem impossible.

God has a plan for our lives, but until our faith is perfected, His plans will often collide with our plans. "'For I know the plans that I have for you,' declares the LORD, 'plans for welfare and not calamity to give you a future and a hope'" (Jeremiah 29:11). Although that passage was given to Israel while in exile, I believe it reveals God's heart for all His chosen people. "But you are a chosen race, a royal priesthood, a holy nation, a people for his own possession, that you may proclaim the excellencies of him who called you out of darkness into his marvelous light. Once you were not a people, but now you are God's people; once you had not received mercy, but now you have received mercy" (1 Peter 2:9-10 ESV).

There are no God-given goals for our lives that can be blocked, uncertain, or impossible. With God all things are possible (Matthew 19:26), and we can do all things through Christ who strengthens us (Philippians 4:13). If God wants it done, it can be done, and whatever God has required us to do, we can do it by the grace of God. The question is, What is included and excluded from "all things"? To answer that question, we need to distinguish between a godly goal and a godly desire. A godly goal is any specific plan or objective that reflects God's purpose for our lives and is not dependent on people or circumstances beyond our right or ability to control.

God's goal for our lives is to become the person He created us to be, "and this is the will of God, your sanctification" (1 Thessalonians 4:3). Nobody or nothing on planet Earth can keep us from becoming the person God created us to be. The only ones who can block that goal is ourselves. People will not always cooperate with our wishes and the circumstances of life will not always be favorable. We never have the absolute right or ability to control others or the circumstances of life. Therefore, if we falsely believe that our identity and our purpose for being here are dependent upon other people or favorable circumstances, we will experience a lot of anger, anxiety, and depression. A godly goal is any plan or objective that depends on the cooperation of other people, the success of events, or favorable circumstances that we have no right or ability to control. Contrast that with a godly desire.

For example, a cashier in the grocery store has to check the price of an item the person in front of you is buying. You're in a hurry and she seems to be moving at the speed of a glacier. You're frustrated with the delay and start to get angry. That "slow poke" is blocking your goal of getting in and out of there fast! But the cashier is not determining who you are. How you respond reveals your flesh patterns and your belief system. Patience is a fruit of the Spirit and if you were walking by the Spirit, it would become evident.

Suppose you're cruising down the interstate, and looking forward to getting home to your family. Suddenly, up ahead you see the dreaded brake lights of hundreds of cars, indicating a traffic jam. With no place to turn off and detour around it, you slam your hand on the steering wheel in anger. Another blocked goal! Your desire to get to a certain place on time may be blocked, but God's goal for you to conform to His image is not being blocked. It is being tested. "The mind of man plans his way, but the LORD directs his steps" (Proverbs 16:9).

Control

Anger is about control or the lack thereof, which is why so many get angry while driving. We leave our "controlled" environment of home and engage the traffic, which we can't control, although we make futile attempts to do so by being passively or actively aggressive. We get angry at government, because we can't control the political system. If your anger toward government is righteous, you actually can do something about it besides voting. You can get involved in grassroots politics and work your way up the system becoming a person of influence. *That would take too long, so I will organize an angry protest and take to the streets.* There are times when a peaceful protest is warranted, but the angry mobs that start riots in order to get their way never end well. You can always pray, speak the truth in love, and be part of the building crew instead of the wrecking crew. Or you can say, *"That is vain! We will follow our own plans, and will every one act according to the stubbornness of his evil heart"* (Jeremiah 18:12 ESV).

Suppose your goal as a parent is to have a loving, harmonious, happy, Christian family. Who can block that goal? Every other member of the family can block that goal, and they all will at some time. That is a legitimate godly desire, but there is no way you can control every member in your family, and if you try, there will be a lot of angry people in your household. However, it is a godly goal to become the spouse and parent God created you to be and nobody can block that goal but yourself.

There is nobody more insecure than a controller. The attempt to control others is based on the false belief that one's success and sense of worth is dependent upon the cooperation of other people and favorable circumstances, which they seek to control. Controllers may not appear angry, but they are seething on the inside, and sadly this will continue all their lives unless they repent, because there is no way they can control everything and everybody.

Consider the boss who believes his job is on the line if his division doesn't accomplish certain goals. To make that happen he tries to control the work of his employees through coercion and intimidation. The result is a workforce driven by fear. Fear is so commonplace in industry that one author wrote a book entitled *Fear, the Corporate F Word.*[8] How many athletes fear the wrath of their coach who believes he must win at all costs in order to be considered successful? How many children fear their angry and controlling parents?

Suppose a pastor wants to use his church to win the neighborhood to Christ. Who can block that goal? Every neighbor can and probably some in the church will. The pastor who is driven to accomplish that goal may unwittingly try to control his congregation and inflict a little guilt on them for not being better witnesses. That is a legitimate desire, but the real goal is to be the pastor God created him to be. Ironically that is the best way to eventually win the neighborhood to Christ.

The intensity with which we react to a particular situation and the longevity of our anger indicates how threatening that person or event appears to us. In other words, how strong and how long our anger persists when a goal is blocked reveals how much we value our objectives. Think about the difference in how you'd feel if you got a flat tire versus being told by your boss that you were a complete failure on your job. The flat tire may have disrupted your plans and prevented you from getting to a certain place on time. You can change the tire or call your roadside service provider and they will change it for you. Annoying as it may be, you will probably get over it in a short time. A stinging reproach of your professional competence or a disruption of your career goals strikes a deeper chord. The anger toward those who leveled such an attack or prevented your promotion would likely cause a few sleepless nights and could even throw you into a tailspin of doubt, debilitating introspection, and depression. Such is the basis for workplace violence.

We have a choice. We can respond according to our old flesh patterns by having an outburst of anger, or we can respond by faith in the power of the Holy Spirit. The fruit of the Spirit is love and that is exhibited by joy, peace, and patience. Instead of getting depressed when a goal seems impossible, we can have the joy of the Lord. Instead of getting anxious when a goal appears to be uncertain, we can have the peace of God that passes all understanding. Instead of anger, we can learn to be patient with people and grow through the trials and tribulations of life.

If the trials and tribulations of life make you angry, then consider Paul's words in Romans 5:3-5: "We also exult in our tribulations, knowing that tribulation brings about perseverance; and perseverance, proven character; and proven character, hope; and hope does not disappoint, because the love of God has been poured out within our hearts through the Holy Spirit who was given to us." The inevitable trials and tribulations of life actually reveal wrong goals, but they make possible God's goal for our life, which is proven character. There is no crisis in life that we cannot grow through.

A suit salesman attended one of Neil's conferences and shared this testimony:

> Your conference has had a profound impact on my life. I was a suit salesman. No, I was an angry suit salesman. I would get so mad if a customer walked away without buying a suit, when I was sure he was going to make a purchase. We had these sales meetings where we

were challenged to set a goal for the number of suits we wanted to sell that week. Prizes were offered if we met or beat our goals. I wanted to be the salesperson of the year and win a trip to Hawaii. To make matters worse, my boss is a Jew and I have been a horrible witness to him. He would have to pull me aside a number of times when I got angry and tell me to settle down. I realized this week that I had the wrong goal. My goal is not to sell a certain number of suits. My goal is to be the suit salesman that God has called me to be. Rather than trying to manipulate and persuade a customer to buy a suit, I began to think of what the customer really needed. I actually talked a customer out of buying a suit that I knew he wouldn't be satisfied with. This simple truth had such a profound impact on my countenance that my boss pulled me aside last night and asked, "Are you all right?" This new-found freedom I feel must have had some effect on my customers, because I sold more suits last week than I ever have before.

What if a godly desire isn't met? We will feel disappointed. But let's face it, life will not always go our way, and people will not always respond to us as they should, but that is not what determines who we are. God has already determined who we are. As children of God, we are in the process of becoming more and more like Jesus, and nobody, or no thing can keep that from happening but ourselves. These disappointments can and should be stepping-stones to greater maturity as the following poem expresses:

"Disappointment – His Appointment,"
    Change one letter, then I see
That the thwarting of my purpose
    Is God's better choice for me.
His appointment must be blessing,

Tho' it may come in disguise,
For the end from the beginning
Open to His wisdom lies.

"Disappointment – His Appointment,"
No good thing will He withhold,
From denials oft we gather
Treasures of His love untold.
Well He knows each broken purpose
Leads to fuller, deeper trust,
And the end of all His dealings
Proves our God is wise and just.

"Disappointment – His Appointment,"
Lord, I take it, then, as such,
Like clay in hands of a potter,
Yielding wholly to Thy touch.
My life's plan is Thy molding;
Not one single choice be mine;
Let me answer, unrepining –
"Father, not my will, but thine."[9]

Edith Lillian Young

Discussion Questions

1. How does the secular world define mental health and how does that square with Christianity?

2. How does the Western worldview that is steeped in rationalism and naturalism conflict with a biblical worldview?

3. What should you do if you are unaware of anything in your past that could be affecting you today? Why?

4. What is the proper way to respond to emotional signals?

5. How is our emotional nature related to our faith?

6. What is God's goal for your life?

7. Explain the difference between a godly goal and a godly desire.

8. What is a major reason people get so angry when driving?

9. What do you have the right to control?

10. What do you have the ability to control?

Steps to Freedom in Christ

Counterfeit Versus Real

The first step toward experiencing your freedom in Christ is to renounce (verbally reject) all involvement (past or present) with occult, cult, or false religious teachings or practices. Participation in any group that denies that Jesus Christ is Lord and/or elevates any teaching or book to the level of (or above) the Bible must be renounced. In addition, groups that require dark, secret initiations, ceremonies, vows, pacts, or covenants need to be renounced. God does not take lightly false guidance. "As for the person who turns to mediums and to spiritists…I will also set My face against that person and will cut him off from among his people" (Leviticus 20:6). Ask God to guide you as follows:

Dear Heavenly Father, please bring to my mind anything and everything that I have done knowingly or unknowingly that involves occult, cult, or false religious teachings and practices. Grant me the wisdom and grace to renounce any

and all spiritual counterfeits, false religious teachings, and
practices. In Jesus's name I pray. Amen.

The Lord may bring events to your mind that you have forgotten, even experiences you participated in as a game or thought was a joke. The purpose is to renounce all counterfeit spiritual experiences and their beliefs that God brings to your mind. Begin this Step by processing the following ten questions:

1. Do you now have, or have you ever had, an imaginary friend, spirit guide, or "angel" offering you guidance or companionship? If it has a name, renounce it by name. **I renounce...**

2. Have you ever seen or been contacted by beings you thought were aliens from another world? Such deceptions should be identified and renounced. **I renounce...**

3. Have you ever heard voices in your head or had repeating, nagging thoughts such as "I'm dumb," "I'm ugly," "Nobody loves me," "I can't do anything right" as if there were a conversation going on inside your head? If so, renounce all deceiving spirits and the lies that you have believed. **I renounce...**

4. Have you ever been hypnotized, attended a New Age seminar, consulted a psychic, medium/channeler, or spiritist? Renounce all specific false prophecies and guidance they offered. **I renounce...**

5. Have you ever made a secret covenant or vow to any organization or persons other than God or made an inner vow contrary to Scripture such as "I will never..."? Renounce all such vows. **I renounce...**

6. Have you ever been involved in a satanic ritual or attended a concert in which Satan was the focus? Renounce Satan and all his works and all his ways. **I renounce…**

7. Have you ever made any sacrifices to idols, false gods, or spirits? Renounce each one. **I renounce…**

8. Have you ever attended any counterfeit religious event or entered a non-Christian shrine that required you to participate in their religious observances such as washing your hands or removing your shoes? Confess your participation and renounce your participation in false worship. **I confess and renounce…**

9. Have you ever consulted a shaman or witch doctor for the purpose of manipulating the spiritual world to place curses, seek psychic healing, or guidance? All such activity needs to be renounced. **I renounce…**

10. Have you ever tried to contact the dead in order to send or receive messages? Renounce such practices. **I renounce…**

Continue this Step using the following *Non-Christian Spiritual Experience Inventory* as a guide. Then pray the prayer following the checklist to renounce each activity or group the Lord brings to mind. He may reveal to you counterfeit spiritual experiences that are not on the list. Be especially aware of your need to renounce non-Christian religious practices that were part of your culture growing up. Prayerfully renounce them *out loud* if you are working through these Steps on your own.

Non-Christian Spiritual Experience Inventory

Check all that you have participated in.

___ Out-of-body experiences

___ Ouija board

___ Blood Mary

___ Charlie Charlie

___ Occult games such as light as a feather

___ Magic eight ball

___ Table or body lifting

___ Spells and curses

___ Mental telepathy/mind control

___ Tarot cards

___ Automatic writing

___ Astrology/horoscopes

___ Palm reading

___ Fortune telling/divination

___ Blood pacts

___ Sexual spirits

___ Séances and circles

___ Trances

___ Spirit guides

___ Clairvoyance

___ Rod and pendulum (dowsing)

___ Hypnosis

___ Wicca

___ Black and white magic/The Gathering

___ Paganism

___ Reiki

___ Channeling/Chakras

___ Reincarnation/previous life healing

___ Mediums and channelers

___ Mormonism

___ Freemasonry

___ Christian Science

___ Church of Scientology

___ Nature worship (Mother Earth)

___ Unitarianism/universalism

___ Hinduism/transcendental meditation

___ Silva Mind Control

___ Buddhism (including Zen)

___ Islam

___ Witchcraft/sorcery

___ Bahaism

___ Spiritism/animism/folk religions

___ Ancestor worship

___ Satanism

Once you have completed your checklist, confess and renounce every false religious practice, belief, ceremony, vow, or pact you were involved in by praying the following prayer aloud. Take your time and be thorough. Give God time to remind you of every specific incident, ritual, etc., as needed:

Dear Heavenly Father, I confess that I have participated in (specifically name every belief and involvement with all that you have checked above), and I renounce them all as counterfeits. I pray that You will fill me with Your Holy Spirit that I may be guided by You. Thank You that in Christ I am forgiven. Amen.

CHAPTER THREE

A WORTHY GOAL

●

Note Paul's persistent wisdom [in Ephesians 4:25-26]. He speaks first to prevent our sinning. If we do not listen, he does not abandon us. His role as a spiritual father does not allow him to give up on us easily. It is like the doctor who tells the sick person what he must do. If the patient refused to hear him, he does not write him off. Rather he continues to care for him by giving him further persuasive counsel. So too does Paul. He has already said, "Do not lie." But suppose anger should arise from lying. He then deals with this. What does he say? "Be angry and do not sin." It is better not to grow angry at all. But if one ever does fall into anger he should at least not be carried away by it toward something worse.

Chrysostom (c. 395)

The tension was overwhelming as I stepped into Byron's office. His wife Marilyn and teenage daughter Meredith were there as well. Meredith was determined to marry Jonathan, a young Christian about eight years her senior. Byron was bound and determined to do everything he could to stop her or die trying. It was the classic "irresistible force" meeting the "unmovable object." Marilyn, a godly woman, was torn between submitting to her husband and not wanting to alienate her daughter. Her story, as told to me, is gut wrenching:

As a family we were in the test of our lives. Mostly responding as things were hurled at us—flaming arrows! Byron was really angry and could not control it. I became angry with him for driving Meredith away. I thought I could be the one to keep these two strong-willed, emotional, stubborn people I loved so much from destroying each other. I could not! So much damage, so many inappropriate actions—ANGRY—so many destructive words—ANGER. I remember screaming at Byron at the top of my voice, "Why won't you stop this!" This was the last time Meredith asked if she could come home. Byron's answer, "Leave Jonathan!"

Meredith was screaming at him, too. I can't believe this memory, such an explosion of emotion. Meredith left home after we found out she was still seeing Jonathan. My husband dared Jonathan to come and face us. Byron lost it with Meredith while Jonathan was on his way over to our house. He got physical with her. The first time ever. Totally out of control. I was petrified. I remember feeling desperate. I couldn't figure out how to defuse Byron. I knew he was going to have a heart attack. I could see his heart beating through his shirt. There was no color in his lips. His eyes were not his. Help God! Meredith was traumatized! I really wondered what would happen to Jonathan when he drove up. Help God!

Byron's goal for his daughter was being blocked and it made him livid. He was angry because of his inability to control his child. Fortunately, God intervened. He stopped trying to undo what he thought was a bad thing and decided to make the best of it. Eventually he came to accept Jonathan and Meredith's marriage.

Several years ago D.L. Thomas and A.J. Weigert conducted research to determine which parenting styles produced the following:

1. Children who have a good self-image and are happy being who they are.

2. Children who conform to the authority of others and have the capacity to get along with their teachers and other authority figures.

3. Children who follow the religious beliefs of their parents, attend the church of their parents, and are likely to continue to do so.

4. Children who identify with the counter-culture, rebelling against the norms of society.[1]

The research was based on two primary parental influences: control and support. Control was defined as the ability to manage a child's behavior. Support was defined as the ability to make a child feel loved. The latter goes beyond simply telling the child that you love them. It means that you are physically and emotionally available in such a way that the child knows that you love them. They identified four different parenting styles, as the diagram on page 64 illustrates.

The *permissive* parent offers high support, but low control. They love the child, but do little to monitor their behavior. The *neglectful* parent provides low control and low support. This parent leaves the child alone to fend for themselves. The *authoritarian* parent seeks to control the child's behavior, but offers little emotional support. The *authoritative* parent loves the child and exercises godly discipline.

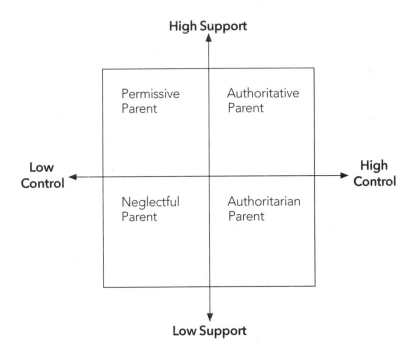

Naturally one would assume that the authoritative parent would produce the best fruit and the research confirmed that. However, the parenting style that was second best in every category was telling. The diagram on page 65 shows how each parenting style ranks in the four categories: sense of worth (SW), conform to authority (CTA), accept parents' religion (APR), rebel against society (REB). Notice that the *permissive* parent ranked second in all categories, and the *neglectful* and *authoritarian* parent tied for the dubious distinction of raising the children most likely to rebel against the establishment, and they shared third and fourth place in the other categories.

The message is clear. The ability to love is more important than the ability to control, and that applies to parenting, education, work, and society in general. The fruit of the Spirit is love, and the love of God is not dependent upon the object. We may not be able to control others, but whether we love them or not is not dependent upon them. It is dependent upon us. It is a measure of our character. The fruit of the Spirit is self-control, not child-control, or spouse-control, or staff-control. When we struggle to manage the behavior of those under our authority, the temptation is to become more authoritarian and that is not the direction a godly leader should go. In our opening story, Byron had made that mistake, and ignored, or was ignorant of Paul's advice in Ephesians 6:4, "Fathers, do not provoke your children to anger, but bring them up in the discipline and instruction of the Lord." Spiritual leaders are instructed to "shepherd the flock of God that is among you, exercising oversight, not under compulsion, but willingly, as God would have you; not for shameful gain, but eagerly; not domineering over those in your charge, but being examples to the flock" (1 Peter 5:2-3 ESV).

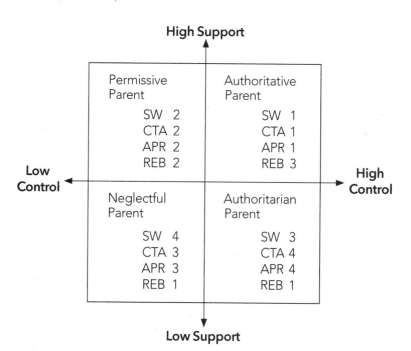

We are not suggesting that you opt for being a permissive leader or parent, but we are saying that ultimately the only one you can control is yourself. A rebellious child is not blocking our goal of being loving parents, but the situation is testing our character. If we respond in the flesh, we are letting subordinates control us, which stands in stark contrast to those who respond in love. "Love is patient and kind; love does not envy or boast; it is not arrogant or rude. It does not insist on its own way; it is not irritable or resentful; it does not rejoice at wrongdoing, but rejoices with the truth. Love bears all things, believes all things, hopes all things, endures all things" (1 Corinthians 13:4-7 ESV).

Godly people in positions of authority have the responsibility to provide leadership and exercise discipline, which is a proof of their love (Hebrews 12:5-11). It is never right, however, to do so in the flesh. Disciplining children in anger is not exercising our God-given authority, it is undermining it. An angry parent may temporarily control the child's behavior, but what is the parent modeling, and what is the lasting effect on the child?

It is required of an elder that he manage his household well, but that must be done "with all dignity" (1 Timothy 3:4 ESV). The best managers in the world have problems as does every good parent. Godly ones just manage it well. The flesh has no dignity. It is mismanagement to say we have no problems or to blame others. Good managers own up to their mistakes, apologize when they respond in the flesh, and grow through the trials and tribulations of life. Such "endurance produces character, and character produces hope, and hope does not put us to shame, because God's love has been poured into our hearts through the Holy Spirit who has been given to us" (Romans 5:4-5 ESV).

Worthy Pursuits

Postmodernism is the age of "What's in it for me?" If you want to be angry the rest of your life then put yourself in the center of life and expect the world to revolve around you. "I" is in the center of pride. Perpetually angry people are self-centered. They are angry at anything or anyone who gets in their way, who disrupts their plans, who blocks their goal of being recognized, rewarded, or first in anything.

Such was the case of the first mention of anger after the fall when the spiritually dead descendants of Adam and Eve were trying to forge a natural life. Cain and Abel acknowledged the existence of God but were not spiritually connected to Him as Adam and Eve were before the fall. Both brought their offering to God. Cain gathered up some grain, but Abel "brought of the firstborn of his flock and of their fat portions. And the LORD had regard for Abel and his offering, but for Cain and his offering he had no regard. So Cain was very angry, and his face fell. The LORD said to Cain, 'Why are you angry, and why has your face fallen? If you do well, will you not be accepted? And if you do not do well, sin is crouching at the door. Its desire is contrary to you, but you must rule over it'" (Genesis 4:4-7 ESV). Cain's goal to be accepted, recognized, and rewarded was blocked. He was so ticked off that he killed his brother.

Every natural person starts their physical existence self-centered. The only world they know is seen from their limited perspective. For all they know, the world revolves around them. Food they dislike is swatted away. They cry in anger when they are dissatisfied. They angrily hit anybody who blocks their selfish pursuits. They pout in a corner when they don't get their own way, or say, "I hate you" to even the best of parents. Pity the mom or dad who continues catering to their desires into the teenage years.

There is one central teaching in all four Gospels that challenges our egocentric ways. Jesus said:

If anyone wishes to come after Me, he must deny himself, and take up his cross daily and follow Me. For whoever wishes to save his life will lose it, but whoever loses his life for My sake, he is the one who will save it. For what is a man profited if he gains the whole world, and loses or forfeits himself? (Luke 9:23-25).

That sounds rather austere, doesn't it? Are we supposed to sell ourselves out to God and give up all our personal goals and desires? Yes! But it's not as sacrificial as it may seem. Hell is where we say, "My will be done." Heaven is where we say, "Thy will be done." Think of the anger and anguish that is gendered when we bite and devour one another to get our way. People who seek to find their identity, purpose, and meaning in their physical, natural, and temporal existence will eventually lose it all. No matter how many toys and trophies we accumulate in the span of our natural life, we can't take it with us. However, those who find new life in Christ will keep it for all eternity. Denying yourself is denying self-rule and acknowledging God as your Creator and Lord. It may seem sacrificial, but what are you actually sacrificing?

You are sacrificing the lower life to gain the higher life. Why people choose to be happy as mortals instead of being blessed as children of God is the mystery of the ages and reveals the hardness of our own hearts. "Delight yourselves in the LORD, and he will give you the desires of your heart" (Psalm 37:4). If you don't first delight yourself in the Lord your desires will be of the flesh, and they cannot be satisfied. But if you first delight yourself in the Lord then your desires will be aligned with God's plan for your life and that is achievable.

You are sacrificing the pleasure of things to gain the pleasures of life. What would you exchange for love, joy, peace, patience, kindness, goodness, faithfulness, gentleness, and self-control? Would you rather have a new car, a second home, a promotion at work, a motorboat, a jug of wine, or a prostitute? There will be a lot of anger if we love things and use people and a lot less anger if we learn to use things to love people. There is nothing inherently wrong with a new car, a better home, or a vacation cabin, but the pleasures don't last and they cannot produce the fruit of the Spirit. How much anger would there be in this world if we all followed Paul's advice in Philippians 2:3-5, "Do nothing from selfish ambition or conceit, but in humility count others more significant than yourselves. Let each of you look not only to his own interests, but also to the interests of others. Have this mind among yourselves, which is yours in Christ Jesus" (esv).

You are sacrificing the temporal to gain the eternal. Some sacrifice! If we fully grasped what was to be gained, we would make it our goal to know God and His ways and live accordingly. Paul wrote, "Discipline yourself for the purpose of godliness; for bodily discipline is only of little profit, but godliness is profitable for all things, since it holds promise for the present life and also for the life to come" (1 Timothy 4:7-8). What value is a great body if your soul is bankrupt? If you shoot for this world you miss the next. If you shoot for the next world you will reap eternal rewards and enjoy the benefits of living a righteous life in this world. Not only will your life be characterized by the fruit of the Spirit, but you will be free to become all that God created you to be, and that is an achievable goal.

We are not saying you shouldn't make plans or set personal goals for your life. However, goals should be understood as a target and not a whip. It's a goal, not a god. The purpose of making plans and setting personal goals is to order our steps today and help us prioritize our time. Having godly goals and desires and following through on them is being a good steward of your time and resources. However, you must be willing to adjust plans that become unrealistic or inconsistent with the leading of the Holy Spirit, because you never know what may happen tomorrow that could temporarily or permanently alter your plans. James warns, "Come now, you who say, 'Today or tomorrow we will go into such and such a town and spend a year there and trade and make a profit'—yet you do not know what tomorrow will bring. What is your life? For you are a mist that appears for a little time and then vanishes. Instead you ought to say, 'If the Lord wills, we will live and do this or that.' As it is you boast in your arrogance. All such boasting is evil" (James 4:13-16 ESV).

Tomorrow the stock market could crash, you could be in an automobile accident, or discover that you have cancer. The world is spinning out of control and there is chaos everywhere, but there is one overarching constant. "Jesus Christ is the same yesterday and today and forever" (Hebrews 13:8). You are His child, and nothing and no one can keep you from being the person God created you to be. "Who shall separate us from the love of Christ? Shall tribulation, or distress, or persecution, or famine, or nakedness, or danger, or sword?...No, in all these things we are more than conquerors through him who loved us" (Romans 8:35,37 ESV). The martyred missionary Jim Elliot wrote, "He is no fool to give up that which he cannot keep in order to gain that which he cannot lose."

Managing Our Life

We wrote in the introduction that anger should be understood from three different perspectives. We haven't yet addressed how flesh patterns are developed and overcome (chapters 5 and 6), and how wounds are healed (chapters 7 and 8). In the next chapter we will consider righteous indignation. How we come to terms with anger on a daily basis is the question at hand.

You start by seeking "first the kingdom of God and his righteousness, and all these things will be added to you" (Matthew 6:33 ESV). If you want to walk by the Spirit and not gratify the desires of the flesh (Galatians 5:16), then you must be filled with (controlled by) the Spirit (Ephesians 5:18). That can only happen when you surrender control of your life to God, resolve all known personal and spiritual conflicts through genuine repentance and faith in God, and trust God's Spirit to direct and empower your life. That is what the *Steps to Freedom in Christ* will help you do. If you hang on to your pride, however, God is opposed to you (James 4:6) and you will not experience the love, joy, peace, and patience that comes from abiding in Christ.

Assuming you are in a right relationship with God, you will still be confronted with daily choices as to what is controlling your life and challenges to right thinking and believing. You always have a choice as to whether you are living by the Spirit or walking by the flesh. Paul wrote in Romans 8:5-9:

> Those who live according to the flesh set their minds on the things of the flesh, but those who live according to the Spirit set their minds on the things of the Spirit. For to set the mind on the flesh is death, but to set the mind on the Spirit is life and peace. For the mind that is set on the flesh is hostile to God, for it does not submit to God's law; indeed it cannot. Those who are in the flesh cannot please God. You, however, are not in the flesh but in the Spirit, if in fact the Spirit of God dwells in you. Anyone who does not have the Spirit of Christ does not belong to him (ESV).

Christians are no longer "in the flesh," as nonbelievers are. Christians are alive "in Christ," but they can choose to live according to their old nature (flesh). We cannot blame another for outbursts of anger. That is a deed of our flesh, not the other person. We need to assume responsibility for such deeds of the flesh the moment we are aware of them. Humble confession is in order. *I'm sorry, I shouldn't have responded that way.* Such honest confession is an agreement with God, and that should be followed with a silent prayer, "Lord, fill me with Your Spirit." There is no need to make that petition public since God knows the thoughts and intentions of the heart. "If we walk in the light, as he is in the light, we have fellowship with one another, and the blood of Jesus his Son cleanses us from all sin" (1 John 1:7 ESV). It is amazing how quickly inward peace is restored if we will just submit to God. It is like spiritual breathing. We "exhale" in confession and "inhale" by being filled with His Spirit. That is how you walk by the Spirit instead of carrying out the desires of the flesh (Galatians 5:16).

Central to this process is the mind, as Paul indicated above. The mind is the control center. You don't do anything without first thinking it. There is always a cause and an effect. It sometimes happens so quickly that it may seem as though you have no will, but you do. Our five senses pick up the data from the environment, which is sent to the brain. The mind assesses the data and that is what determines the signal that is sent from the central nervous system to the peripheral nervous system. You have no control over the peripheral nervous system, but you do have control of how you interpret the data. You have control over how you think and what you believe. Dr. Gary Chapman describes how the body responds to an angry assessment:

> The body's nervous system "gets the adrenaline flowing." Depending upon the level of anger any or all of the following may happen physically. The adrenal glands release two hormones: epinephrine (adrenaline) and norepinephrine (noradrenaline). These two chemicals seem to give people the arousal, the tenseness, the excitement, the heat of anger. These hormones in turn stimulate changes in heart rate, blood pressure, lung function,

and digestive tract activity which further add to the general arousal feelings people have when they are angry. It is these physiological changes that give people the feeling of being overwhelmed by anger and unable to control it.[2]

The intense physiological reactions produced by our adrenal glands can deceive us into thinking our anger is beyond our control and that we have to give in to it. That is simply not true. Recall God's words to Cain when he allowed anger to manifest, "Sin is crouching at the door; and its desire is for you, but you must master it." Cain didn't, and he killed his brother.

You master it by winning the battle for your mind as Paul instructs us to do. "Let your reasonableness be known to everyone. The Lord is at hand; do not be anxious [double-minded] about anything, but in everything by prayer and supplication with thanksgiving let your requests be made known to God. And the peace of God, which surpasses all understanding, will guard your hearts and your minds in Christ Jesus" (Philippians 4:5-7 ESV).

In other words, don't be double-minded about anything. If you set your mind on the flesh, you will live according to the flesh. The key is to practice threshold thinking. The moment a thought comes to your mind, take it captive to the obedience of Christ (2 Corinthians 10:5). If it is not consistent with the ways of God, ignore it. God will guard our hearts and our minds if we turn to Him, but we must also assume our responsibility as Paul directs, "Finally, brothers, whatever is true, whatever is honorable, whatever is just, whatever is pure, whatever is lovely, whatever is commendable, if there is any excellence, if there is anything worthy of praise, think about these things" (Philippians 4:8 ESV).

Your prayer can be silent and simple like, "God, help me." He will, but you must assume responsibility for your own thoughts and then put them into action. Believe what is true, do what is honorable, just, pure, lovely, and commendable then "the God of peace will be with you" (4:9). Peace comes when you are a doer of the Word, and not just a hearer (James 1:22). Setting your minds on the Spirit, and setting "your minds on things that are above, not on things that are on earth" (Colossians 3:2 ESV) leads to righteous living. "Faith apart from works is useless" (James 2:20 ESV).

In Matthew 5:21-22, Jesus teaches that genuine righteousness is not achievable by external conformity to a law, but by the inner transformation of the heart:

> You have heard that the ancients were told, "You shall not commit murder" and "Whoever commits murder shall be liable to the court." But I say to you that everyone who is angry with his brother shall be guilty before the court; and whoever shall say to his brother, "You good-for-nothing" shall be guilty before the supreme court; and whoever says, "You fool," shall be guilty enough to go into the fiery hell.

We don't believe Jesus said that to condemn us or we would all be condemned to hell. He is revealing how dangerous anger can be and how we can avoid destroying one another. To control our anger, we have to assume responsibility for our thoughts. The anger is there because we have mentally processed the data that our physical senses have picked up. We do have the capacity to choose what we are going to do with that information, and by choosing the truth we will control our emotional response of anger. Often when we see another person emotionally overcome, we want to grab hold of the person and say, "Think. Put this in perspective. Get hold of yourself." We need to talk to ourselves the same way.

Anger that festers and boils within us is letting the sun go down on our anger, giving the devil an opportunity (Ephesians 4:26-27) to operate his divide-and-conquer and search-and-destroy mission (1 Peter 5:8). It results in angry words that grieve the Holy Spirit (Ephesians 4:29-30). It decays into "bitterness and wrath and anger…along with all malice" (Ephesians 4:31).

Not everything can be blamed on the flesh, however. The battle for our minds may have a spiritual origin as Paul clearly warned in 1 Timothy 4:1, "But the Spirit explicitly says that in later times some will fall away from the faith, paying attention to deceitful spirits and doctrines of demons." "But I am afraid that, as the serpent deceived Eve by his craftiness, your minds will be led astray from the simplicity and purity of devotion to Christ" (2 Corinthians 11:3). We have seen the evidence of this all over the world in thousands of instances of leading people through the *Steps to Freedom in Christ*. Regardless of the source, we need to take "every thought captive to the obedience of Christ" (2 Corinthians 10:5).

Standing Firm

Living in a fallen world is an ongoing test of our resolve to live a godly life. The challenge is to "not be overcome by evil, but overcome evil with good" (Romans 12:21). When confronted by evil, can we maintain our position in Christ and not violate the fruit of the Spirit, or do we respond in the flesh? Are we going to let other people determine who we are? God is the only One who has that right. The world is becoming more hostile. That doesn't change who we are in Christ. There are wars and rumors of wars. We are still children of God. The world is going to hell. We're not. The stock market could crash again. Our God will meet all our needs according to His riches. We could be imprisoned for our beliefs, and we would still be free "in Christ." Satan has deceived the whole world, but the truth has set us free. There is nothing the devil can do about our identity and position in Christ, but if he can convince us to disbelieve what God says is true about us, we will live as though it isn't.

Even the best of people will disappoint us at times. We can respond in kind, or we can take the high road and become more like Christ. When we screw up, we hope that others will cut us some slack and offer us a second chance. We all need to follow the Golden Rule and treat others the same way we want them to treat us (Matthew 7:12). Bob Benson captured that essence in the following quote:

> He promised he would, but he didn't. He'd said he could, but he couldn't.
>
> He's let me down, put me off, he had it coming—so I gave it to him—skillfully, enthusiastically, I let him have it.
>
> And then a part of me, the part that's made of earth said "at'ta boy, that's telling him, that'll get him moving—that's the old business drive—plenty of push-hustle—you sure showed him."
>
> And then another part of me, a part that's made like God whispered soft and clear, "You showed him all right—you showed him everything—everything, that is, but forbearance, kindness, forgiveness, longsuffering—in short, everything—but Christlikeness."
>
> "But he had it coming, he got what he deserved," the earth was quick to say.
>
> "But remember Christ," the image replied. You failed Him, broke your promises. You missed the mark, you deserved judgment, but you needed mercy.
>
> "He gave you what you needed instead of what you deserved."
>
> Now the struggles ceased—both voices bowed in prayer:

> *Oh God—make me sensitive not to what people deserve, but rather to their needs. Make me like Christ.*[3]

Discussion Questions

1. Why do we insist on having our way, that we are right and others are wrong?

2. What did you learn from the research on styles of parenting?

3. Why does love "not insist on its own way"?

4. What do good managers do and not do?

5. What is right or wrong about setting goals and making plans?

6. Why is it so difficult to surrender our will to God's will?

7. What's in it for you if you deny yourself?

8. What one major choice do you have when responding to the challenges of life? How do you make that choice?

9. Where is the battle for control being waged? How do you win that battle?

10. How do you keep others from controlling who you are and how you respond to them?

Steps to Freedom in Christ

Pride Versus Humility

Pride comes before a fall, but God gives grace to the humble (James 4:6; 1 Peter 5:1-10). Humility is confidence properly placed in God, and we are instructed to "put no confidence in the flesh"

(Philippians 3:3). We are to be "strong in the Lord and in the strength of His might" (Ephesians 6:10). Proverbs 3:5-7 urges us to trust in the Lord with all our hearts and to not lean on our own understanding. Use the following prayer to ask for God's guidance:

> *Dear Heavenly Father, You have said that pride goes before destruction and an arrogant spirit before stumbling. I confess that I have focused on my own needs and desires and not those of others. I have not always denied myself, picked up my cross daily, and followed You. I have relied on my own strength and resources instead of resting in Yours. I have placed my will before Yours and centered my life around myself instead of You. I confess my pride and selfishness and pray that all ground gained in my life by the enemies of the Lord Jesus Christ would be canceled as I repent and overcome these sinful flesh patterns. I choose to rely upon the Holy Spirit's power and guidance so that I will do nothing from selfishness or empty conceit. With humility of mind, I choose to regard others as more important than myself. I acknowledge You as my Lord and confess that apart from You I can do nothing of lasting significance. Please examine my heart and show me the specific ways I have lived my life in pride. In the gentle and humble name of Jesus I pray. Amen.* (See Proverbs 16:18; Matthew 6:33; 16:24; Romans 12:10; Philippians 2:3.)

Pray through the list below and use the prayer following to confess any sins of pride the Lord brings to mind.

___ Having a stronger desire to do my will than God's will

___ Leaning too much on my own understanding and experience rather than seeking God's guidance through prayer and His Word

___ Relying on my own strengths and resources instead of depending on the power of the Holy Spirit

___ Being more concerned about controlling others than in developing self-control

___ Being too busy doing "important" and selfish things rather than seeking and doing God's will

___ Having a tendency to think that I have no needs

___ Finding it hard to admit when I am wrong

___ Being more concerned about pleasing people than pleasing God

___ Being overly concerned about getting the credit I feel I deserve

___ Thinking I am more humble, spiritual, religious, or devoted than others

___ Being driven to obtain recognition by attaining degrees, titles, and positions

___ Often feeling that my needs are more important than another person's needs

___ Considering myself better than others because of my academic, artistic, athletic, or other abilities and accomplishments

___ Not waiting on God

___ Other ways I have thought more highly of myself than I should

For each of the above areas that has been true in your life, pray:

Dear Heavenly Father, I agree I have been proud by (name what you checked above). Thank You for Your forgiveness. I choose to humble myself before You and others. I choose to place all my confidence in You and put no confidence in my flesh. In Jesus's name I pray. Amen.

CHAPTER FOUR

RIGHTEOUS INDIGNATION

●

There is a just and also an unjust anger...The unjust anger...is to be restrained in man—lest he should rush into some very great evil through rage. This type of anger cannot exist in God. There is also just anger. This anger is necessary in man for the correction of wickedness. Plainly, then, it is necessary in God, who sets an example for man. Just as we should restrain those who are subject to our power, so also God should restrain the offenses of everyone. It is the fear of God alone that guards the mutual society of men. By this, life itself is sustained, protected, and governed. However, such fear is taken away if man is persuaded that God is without anger. For not only the common advantage, but also reason and truth itself, persuade us that He is moved and is indignant when unjust actions are done.

Lactantius (c. 304-313)

I was leading a group through the *Steps to Freedom in Christ* at the conclusion of a Living Free in Christ conference, which has now become the Freedom in Christ Discipleship Course. We came to the Step entitled "Submission Versus Rebellion." As I was explaining the Step, a middle-aged lady stood up and angrily said, "How can I be submissive to our government that just passed a law endorsing same sex-marriage?" The last thing I wanted was a debate on the floor at a time when most were doing serious business with God. I often look for some comic relief during such times, partly to stall for time while I'm thinking of a good answer. Besides, we should be slow to speak and slow to anger. Since I was in Canada at the time and not very fond of our president, I said, "Well, ma'am, if you would be open to swapping your prime minister for our president, I would be open to that."

Fortunately there was enough laughter to give me the time to think of a good response. I said, "According to the thirteenth chapter of Romans, we are to be submissive to governing authorities, for there is no authority except from God, and those that exist have been instituted by God. We would have nothing but social chaos if everyone disobeyed governing authorities they disagreed with. Is it okay with you if your children disobey you when they disagree with you? Although we are in agreement about the definition of marriage, we can't be rebellious against governing authorities and expect God to work through us to correct that which is wrong. When Esther was informed that all Jews were to be killed, she called for three days of prayer and fasting before she approached the king who was her husband. Because of her humble submission the nation of Israel was saved." The lady relented and sat down, but she was probably still smoldering with righteous indignation. What, if anything, could she do about it?

Righteous indignation is a justifiable reaction to the things that anger God, motivating us to confront injustices by taking appropriate action. Jesus demonstrated that when He cleansed the temple, saying, "It is written, 'My house shall be called a house of prayer'; but you are making it a robbers' den" (Matthew 21:13). Jesus was angry at the defamation of God's glory in His temple, and He did something about it. However, if you want to get angry and not sin, then get angry the way Christ did. Get angry at sin. He turned over the tables, not the moneychangers.

On the Sabbath, Jesus entered into the synagogue and saw a man with a withered hand. His enemies watched to see if He would do anything that would conflict with their traditions. They remained silent, however, when Jesus asked, "Is it lawful to do good or to do harm on the Sabbath, to save a life or to kill?" (Mark 3:4). The Lord looked "around at them with anger, grieved at their hardness of heart," and proceeded to heal the man (Mark 3:5). Jesus exposed their religious hypocrisy while maintaining complete control of Himself and the situation. By asking the question, He let them self-incriminate. He was not responding to a blocked goal, because God has no blocked goals. The wrath of God is part of His righteous nature. It will become part of our nature if we are growing in Christ, because we are partakers of His divine nature (2 Peter 1:4).

New believers are beginning the process of becoming holy as He is holy. Their moral authority is limited by their lack of maturity. That was the case for the church at Corinth, which tolerated some gross immorality. Paul said, "I, brothers, could not address you as spiritual people, but as people of the flesh, as infants in Christ. I fed you with milk, not solid food, for you were not ready for it. And even now you are not yet ready, for you are still of the flesh" (1 Corinthians. 3:1-3 ESV). Paul was not scolding them because they were carnal infants in Christ, but because they were still carnal when they should have matured. Immature Christians lack the discernment necessary to take responsible action when the lines between good and evil are blurred. "Solid food is for the mature, for those who have their powers of discernment trained by constant practice to distinguish good from evil" (Hebrews 5:14 ESV). We must choose wisely those who would lead us. An elder "must not be a recent convert, or he may become puffed up with conceit and fall into the condemnation of the devil" (1 Timothy 3:6 ESV). Look at the protests that take place on college campuses fueled by liberal professors who know nothing of God. Their cause is questionable at best, and their behavior is often carnal,[1] and sometimes criminal.

That does not mean that a young believer can't stand for righteousness and speak up when injustices occur. They can and should, but there are limits to what they can accomplish. Movements that confront major social injustices like abortion need wise-godly leaders who are less likely to default to flesh patterns when under fire. They know how to marshal the forces, organize prayer support, and train the uninitiated. It may take years, decades, and even centuries to overcome social injustices.

Righteous anger that does not result in righteous action often leads to cynicism. The kingdom of God doesn't need any more cynics who only sit in judgment of others. Righteous indignation should lead us to do something constructive—to forgive, pray, alleviate suffering or oppression, or campaign for justice.

I have traveled to Colombia, South America, many times, where revolutionary forces have battled the government for 40 years. What started out as a legitimate protest fueled by anger against the corruption in government had degenerated into a revolutionary army that terrorized the country. Initially it was probably a just cause that lacked mature leadership. Drugs, extortion, and hostage taking became their financial means of support.

In contrast, the city of Cali, Colombia, was blighted by a drug cartel until a godly doctor organized the local Christian community to meet in a soccer stadium for all night prayer vigils. The doctor was martyred but the Cali cartel doesn't exist anymore. I happened to have been in Bogota, Colombia, when there was a peaceful demonstration. It was instigated by college students who organized a global protest against the revolutionaries for the purpose of making the statement that they do not support their revolutionary efforts. It was a peaceful assembly of over a million people during the noon hour. Young people can make a righteous stand. Peaceful negotiations are now underway to end the struggle, and the roads are again safe to travel in Colombia.

Gandhi's peaceful protest in India was the model for the Martin Luther King Jr.-led civil rights movement. They were both martyred for their efforts. There is always a price to pay for freedom.

Nelson Mandala had every right to be angry over apartheid and his imprisonment, but he channeled that energy for the good of the country. After prison he became a moderate voice of reason and won the Nobel Peace Prize for being a peacemaker.

There is a right way and a wrong way to stand up and let our voices be heard when sin is running amuck. What is more atrocious than aborting babies? Godly mothers don't kill their offspring. Public support, however, declines when an abortion clinic gets bombed and an abortionist doctor gets killed by a zealot ruled by his flesh. Protests arranged against abortion clinics aren't effective when one can't tell the difference between those who are pro-choice and those who are pro-life unless you read the signs. Succumbing to the flesh and responding to the opposition with outbursts of anger and vitriolic speech will not be successful. A silent protest staged by praying Christians at abortion clinics would have been more successful.

The logic is similar to Peter's advice to wives who have disobedient husbands. "Likewise, wives, be subject to your own husbands, so that even if some do not obey the word, they may be won without a word by the conduct of their wives...when they see your respectful and pure conduct...let your adorning be the hidden person of the heart with the imperishable beauty of a gentle and quiet spirit, which in God's sight is precious" (1 Peter 3:1,2,4 ESV).

Being Salt and Light

The beatitudes (Matthew 5:3-11) are an encouragement to the

humble minority who live in a world that "lies in the power of the evil one" (1 John 5:19 ESV). There are injustices everywhere. *Blessed are the poor in spirit*, because they are aware of their need of forgiveness and new life in Christ. Theirs is the kingdom of God. *Blessed are those who mourn* because of the sinfulness of humanity, because Jesus came to bind up the brokenhearted, set captives free and "to comfort all who mourn" (Isaiah 61:2). *Blessed are the meek*, who have great strength under great control. They don't respond in the flesh. They shall inherit the earth. *Blessed are they who hunger and thirst after righteousness*. They will be satisfied with the fruit of the Spirit. *Blessed are the merciful, for they shall receive mercy*. They give others what they need, and not what they deserve. *Blessed are the pure in heart, for they shall see God* and His handiwork when others are not even aware of His presence. *Blessed are the peacemakers, for they shall be called sons of God*. Believers and nonbelievers alike recognize their good works and calming influence on society and award Nobel Peace Prizes to people like Mother Teresa. *Blessed are those who are persecuted for righteousness sake, for theirs is the kingdom of God*. Their unwavering stand on moral issues is doing kingdom work. They will be reviled, persecuted, and falsely accused, but their reward is great in heaven. Such people are the salt of the earth and the light of the world (Matthew 5:13-14). God works through them (us) to restrain the evil forces that corrupt the world. Being motivated by righteous indignation to overcome evil with good is how we function as salt and light in this world.

How can we restore saltiness to the salt (verse 13), and put our lights on a stand (verse 14)? First, we have to look in the mirror. Judgment begins in the household of God. That is where Jesus started when He cleansed the temple. John the Baptist confronted Herod, a Jewish leader, not Pontius Pilate, a surrogate of secular Rome. The atrocities of the Crusades are still considered a blight on church history. The Reformation was essential for correcting church practices, but thousands were slaughtered afterward by carnal "Christians." Apartheid was supported by the Reformed Church in South Africa. The Orthodox Church stood silently by while Stalin and Lenin ravaged the people of Russia. Catholics were part of the liberation theology that plagued South America and also covered up the sins of child-molesting priests around the world. Southern Protestants supported slavery before the Civil War, and many churches were still practicing racial discrimination a century later.

We can't preach the good news and be the bad news. We have to take the log out of our own eye before we notice the speck that is in our brother's eye (Matthew 7:3). It is hypocritical to speak out against social ills while our own sins are being exposed. "Judge not," Jesus said, "that you will be not judged" (Matthew 7:1).

Second, turn to God in prayer the moment your anger is aroused by the injustices around you. I was playing golf with three Christian friends right across the street from Columbine High School in Colorado when 12 students and a teacher were killed by two rebellious students. Ironically we saw it on TV in the clubhouse after nine holes. We stood on the tenth green, held hands, and prayed. There is no more effective way of channeling righteous anger than having a prayer vigil during and following senseless tragedies.

Paul wrote, "First of all, then, I urge that supplications, prayers, intercessions, and thanksgiving be made for all people, for kings and all who are in high positions, that we may lead a peaceful and quiet life, godly and dignified in every way. This is good, and it is pleasing in the sight of God our Savior, who desires all people to be saved and to come to the knowledge of the truth" (1 Timothy 2:1-4 ESV). Rather than be rebellious to governing authorities, we are to pray for them that they would be instruments for justice, and those who need justice would come to a saving knowledge of our Lord Jesus Christ.

In Calgary, Canada, a group of pastors took this seriously. City officials have a huge responsibility and often feel the heat from the public. Police, paramedics, and firefighters are in constant danger. So two representative pastors made an appointment with the mayor who was not a believer. He probably had his guard up when they came. He was surprised when they asked for a list of all their police and fire personnel so their church members could pray for them, their safety, and their families. The mayor immediately told his assistant to give them what they wanted. The pastors went to council members and asked how they could pray for them and their families individually. One female member was a self-proclaiming liberal and told them so. A year later her voting took a decisive turn when she became a believer.

Jesus said, "But I say to you who hear, love your enemies, do good to those who hate you, bless those who curse you, pray for those who abuse you" (Luke 6:27-28 ESV). That is humanly impossible when you are filled with righteous indignation, because of their unrighteous behavior toward you. It is not impossible for God, however, because His love is not dependent upon the object. He loves us, because God is love. It is His nature to love us and others, which is why it is unconditional. "If you love those who love you, what benefit is that to you? For even sinners love those who love them" (Luke 6:32 ESV).

In order to love your enemy you need to be filled with God's Holy Spirit. Then you may be able to act kindly to those who hate you, bless (speak well of) those who curse you, and pray for those who abuse you like Jesus did on the cross. "Father forgive them; for they know not what they do" (Luke 23:34 KJV). Spirit-filled believers don't let their enemies determine who they are or succumb to their provocations by responding in a carnal way. That is Holy Spirit-enabled love and self-control.

Third, be a silent witness. God is omnipresent and "He...will convict the world concerning sin and righteousness and judgment" (John 16:8). We don't have to do that. If your children are misbehaving, you don't have to say anything when you walk in their room. They are caught and conviction is written all over their faces. Let yourself be known as a Christian, where you live, work, and play without being obnoxious. Sinners loved to be around Jesus, and He was most upset with religious hypocrisy. If you are glorifying God in your body then God's presence is being manifested wherever you are. Some may not choose to work or play with you because your presence is too convicting. You also may be attacked for your godly life (1 Peter 4:4).

When the cat's away the mice will play, but the hidden effect of just being present is also affecting the spiritual realm. Discerning Christians can meet another believer for the first time and sense a compatible spirit. Like spirits attract. Opposing spirits repel. I have approached people who are under Satan's influence and they depart without saying anything. The demonic spirit harassing them is reacting to the Holy Spirit within me. I have seen people who are seeking freedom push their chairs away from me and recoil when touched. When we train encouragers to use the *Steps to Freedom in Christ*, we instruct them not to touch someone in spiritual bondage until they are free. Then they have a compatible spirit and want to be hugged. Don't overlook the value of the church's physical and spiritual presence in this world. Wherever and whenever the church is strong, there has been an elevation of social justice and a decline when the church is absent or acting carnal.

Four, use assertive anger to stand up for righteousness when directed by God. The only thing that has to happen in order for sin to abound is for good people to do nothing. There are two major questions that need to be asked before action is initiated: "Do we have the right and the ability to make a difference?" and "Who is ultimately responsible?"

It is never right to do wrong even though it may appear that some good may come of it. The end does not justify the means. It may seem good that the abortion doctor who was killed could no longer terminate pregnancies, but it tarnished the reputation and efforts of responsible saints who have prayed and worked for years to overturn *Roe v. Wade*. It is a test of our character to never compromise ourselves in order to win. Do we really believe that we can overcome evil with good in a world that believes nice people finish last? Probably not if we think that just one act of kindness would do it. It takes a lifestyle of consistent living to influence others, but what really stumps the unrighteous is when they observe how well we hold up under fire, grow through the trials and tribulations of life, and fearlessly face death with dignity.

Other than the grace exhibited by Jesus on the cross there is probably no better example of assertive anger than the speech and subsequent stoning of Stephen. The Pharisees could not withstand the wisdom and the Spirit with which he was speaking. So they secretly instigated some men to tell lies about him, and Stephen was brought before the council. "And gazing at him, all who sat in the council saw that his face was like the face of an angel" (Acts 6:15 esv). That is grace under fire. After his Holy Spirit-inspired speech the council was "enraged, and they ground their teeth at him. But he, full of the Holy Spirit, gazed into heaven and saw the glory of God, and Jesus standing at the right hand of God" (Acts 7:54-55 esv). Scripture teaches that Jesus is seated at the right hand of the Father, so what do you think it meant to Stephen when he saw Jesus *standing* at the right hand of the Father cheering him on? We can imagine God the Father saying of Stephen, "That's my son!"

That is a God we want to serve and are willing to die for.

Not everybody would have the ability to give the speech Stephen made in Acts 7, much less the courage to do it. We should always be able to speak the truth in love, but there are certain injustices that require other abilities, such as having an in-depth understanding of the issues and being in positions of authority. Rather than reveal our ignorance when angered by injustices, it is often wise to bring in the experts. The larger Christian community has legal experts, apologists, scientists, and philosophers who have been raised up to fight for righteousness and speak out against injustices. It is usually best not to make a stand if one is poorly informed on the subject. It is, however, right to share your discernment when you sense that something is wrong.

It is every believer's responsibility to be a positive witness and speak the truth in love, but we should do so without usurping God's role. We believe that God has drawn a line as follows:

God's Sovereignty | Human Responsibility

Everything on the left of the line is God's responsibility. Everything on the right side of the line is our responsibility. It is our responsibility to believe, but we can't save ourselves. We can be creative, but we can't create something out of nothing. We are commanded not to judge one another, but we are instructed to carry out church discipline. Judgment is a matter of character, and discipline is a matter of behavior. Calling someone a liar is judging them. They will likely become defensive and their battle is now with us, when it should be with God. The moment we usurp the role of the Holy Spirit in other people's lives we misdirect their battle with God onto ourselves, and we are not up for the task.

Discipline is based on observed behavior. If we confront someone who has told a lie, it is better to say, "What you just said is not true." That is not judging them, and it doesn't interfere with God's role of convicting them of sin. It is just holding them accountable. "Brothers, if anyone is caught in any transgression, you who are spiritual should restore him in a spirit of gentleness" (Galatians 6:1 ESV). Discipline is different from punishment. Punishment is solely focused on past behavior. Good parents don't spank a child as a form of punishment. They lovingly discipline in order to extinguish bad behavior and to superintend future choices. "For the moment all discipline seems painful rather than pleasant, but later it yields the peaceful fruit of righteousness to those who have been trained by it" (Hebrews 12:11 ESV).

On the right side of the line, there are various realms of human responsibilities depending upon who has the authority to carry out the rule of law. One division is between the church and the state. The church is the conscience of the state, but not the executor of the state. The Bible is the sole authority of the church, but not the state, which is governed in the United States by the Constitution. Jesus was asked by the Pharisees, "'Is it lawful to pay taxes to Caesar, or not?' But Jesus, aware of their malice, said, 'Why put me to the test, you hypocrites? Show me the coin for the tax.' And they brought him a denarius. And Jesus said to them, 'Whose likeness and inscription is this?' They said, 'Caesar's.' Then he said to them, 'Therefore render to Caesar the things that are Caesar's, and to God the things that are God's'" (Matthew 22:17-21 ESV).

The church has the right and responsibility to carry out church discipline, but not over those who are outside the faith. The state has the right and the responsibility to carry out the rule of law, but they do not have the right to tell us what to believe. When the state oversteps their authority we must obey God rather than man. Tensions arise when the state interferes with church and family responsibilities: telling pastors what they can or cannot preach or usurping the role of a parent. We need to make our voices heard, but the long-term strategy is to encourage more believers to become judges, mayors, governors, and presidents. Writing letters to our government representatives, signing petitions, and marching for life has some merit but pales in comparison to the influence a godly person has who is working within the system behind closed doors. God has His people everywhere, and we need to unite behind them in prayer. Whoever wrote the serenity prayer had it right. "*God, grant me the serenity to accept the things I cannot change. The courage to change the things I can, and the wisdom to know the difference. Amen.*"

Discussion Questions

1. What determines whether anger is right or wrong?

2. Why must we be in submission to governing authorities?

3. What is the purpose of righteous indignation? Why did God create us to have such anger?

4. What are the right and wrong ways to stand up against social injustices?

5. Why does judgment begin in the household of God?

6. Why and how should we pray when moved by righteous indignation?

7. What can be accomplished by being a silent witness? When is it not enough?

8. What are the rights and wrongs of assertive anger?

9. What are the risks of asserting righteous anger?

10. Why is it important to know what our rights and responsibilities are and the scopes and limits of church, state, and personal authority?

Steps to Freedom in Christ

Rebellion Versus Submission

We live in rebellious times. Many people sit in judgment of those in authority over them, and they submit only when it is convenient, or they do so in the fear of being caught. The Bible instructs us to pray for those in authority over us (1 Timothy 2:1-2) and submit to governing authorities (Romans 13:1-7). Rebelling against God and His established authority leaves us spiritually vulnerable. The only time God permits us to disobey earthly leaders is when they require us to do something morally wrong or attempt to rule outside the realm of their authority. To have a submissive spirit and servant's heart, pray the following prayer:

> *Dear Heavenly Father, You have said that rebellion is like the sin of witchcraft and arrogance like the evil of idolatry (see 1 Samuel 15:23). I know that I have not always been submissive, but instead have rebelled in my heart against You and against those You have placed in authority over me in attitude and in action. Please show me all the ways I have been rebellious. I choose now to adopt a submissive spirit and a servant's heart. In Jesus's name I pray. Amen.*

It is an act of faith to trust God to work in our lives through something less than perfect leaders, but that is what God is asking us to do. Should those in positions of leadership or power abuse their authority and break the laws designed to protect innocent people, you need to seek help from a higher authority. Many governments require certain types of abuse to be reported to a governmental agency. If that is your situation, we urge you to get the help you need immediately. Don't, however, assume that someone in authority is violating God's Word just because he or she is telling you to do something you don't like. God has set up specific lines of authority to protect us and give order to society. It is the position of authority that we respect. Without governing authorities, every society would be chaos. From the list below, allow God to show you any specific ways you have been rebellious and use the prayer that follows to confess those sins He brings to mind.

> Civil government (including traffic laws, tax laws, attitude toward government officials) (Romans 13:1-7; 1 Timothy 2:1-4; 1 Peter 2:13-17)
>
> Parents, stepparents, or legal guardians (Ephesians 6:1-3)
>
> Teachers, coaches, school officials (Romans 13:1-4)
>
> Employers (past and present) (1 Peter 2:18-23)
>
> Husband (1 Peter 3:1-4) or wife (Ephesians 5:21; 1 Peter 3:7) (Note to husbands: Ask the Lord if your lack of love for your wife could be fostering a rebellious spirit within her. If so, confess that as a violation of Ephesians 5:22-33.)
>
> Church leaders (Hebrews 13:7)
>
> God (Daniel 9:5,9)

For each way in which the Spirit of God brings to your mind that you have been rebellious, use the following prayer to specifically confess that sin:

> *Heavenly Father, I confess that I have been rebellious toward (name or position) by (specifically confess what you did or did not do). Thank You for Your forgiveness. I choose to be submissive and obedient to Your Word. In Jesus's name I pray. Amen.*

CHAPTER FIVE

MENTAL STRONGHOLDS

●

It is absurd for those who being led toward the kingdom of God to have sin ruling over them or for those who are called to reign with Christ to choose to be captives to sin, as if one should throw down the crown from off his head and choose to be the slave of a hysterical woman who comes begging and covered in rags…How is it that sin can reign in you? It is not from any power of its own but only from your laziness.

Chrysostom, *Homilies on Romans* (c. 395)

Every day we face challenges that threaten our inner peace, that block our goals, that alter our plans, but we have a choice. We can live by the Spirit or walk by the flesh. We can choose the truth or believe a lie. Learning how to live dependently upon God is how we maintain self-control on a daily basis. We pick up our cross daily and follow Him.

Chronic anger, however, may have its roots in the past as the following request for help illustrates:

> I have struggled with anger all my life, since I was a little boy. My peers always picked on me and my dad constantly criticized everything I did. I have come a long way. However, it seems that there are still some strongholds in my mind over this area. I get really upset if I am mistreated or disrespected by people, especially family

> members. I don't hold grudges for as long as I used to, but there still appears to be some block in the process of forgiveness. I react so quickly with outbursts of anger that I don't even realize where they come from or the reason behind them. My wife tells me if I'm mad to "get happy," as if we have direct control over our feelings like that. I know that the problem is in my mind, but the negative thoughts appear so buried that I don't even know they are there. Pray that God would reveal the root causes of this bondage to me.

Every Jesus follower has some negative history of neglect, abuse, rejection, criticism, and a myriad of interpersonal conflicts, but that wasn't the case for the first couple. God created Adam and Eve in His image and His likeness. "God blessed them," and spoke to them personally (Genesis 1:28). Adam and Eve were *secure* in the Father's provision of their safety, food, and shelter (Genesis 1:29), and they were never alone (Genesis 2:18). They were *accepted* by God and one another. "The man and his wife were both naked and were not ashamed" (Genesis 2:25). They had nothing to hide and nothing to cover up. They could have intimate relationships with each other in the presence of God. Finally, they were *significant*, because God had given them dominion over all the earth (Genesis 1:28)! Since there were no unmet needs, no frustrations, no blocked goals, and no sense of injustice, there was no anger. Adam and Eve lived in perfect peace with God and each other.

Suddenly Paradise was shattered and their attributes became our needs. They ate fruit from the tree of the knowledge of good and evil, which God had expressly forbidden them to do (Genesis 2:17). Eve was deceived by the serpent to believe there was something she needed outside of God's will. Adam chose to sin (1 Timothy 2:14); and "through the one man's disobedience the many were made sinners" (Romans 5:19). Immediately, Adam and Eve felt fear, shame, and guilt and the only cause was their sin that separated them from God. They covered their nakedness with fig leaves, wanting to hide from God's presence among the trees of the garden (Genesis 3:7-8).

Adam and Eve were created to be physically and spiritually alive. Physical life is the union of our soul with our body. Physical death for the believer is to be absent from the body and to be present with the Lord. Spiritual life is the union of our soul with God. God had warned, "In the day that you eat from [the fruit of the tree of the knowledge of good and evil] you shall surely die" (Genesis 2:17). They died spiritually. They no longer were in union with God. Physical death would be a consequence of their sin as well, but not for hundreds of years. The first emotion expressed by Adam was fear, because there is nothing more frightening than to be abandoned and totally alone.

As a result of their sin, every one of their descendants will be born physically alive but spiritually dead. Paul explains our spiritual condition apart from Christ in Ephesians 2:1-3:

> You were dead in your trespasses and sins, in which you
> formerly walked according to the course of this world,
> according to the prince of the power of the air, of the
> spirit that is now working in the sons of disobedience.
> Among them we too all formerly lived in the lusts of our
> flesh, indulging the desires of the flesh and of the mind,
> and were by nature children of wrath, even as the rest.

Having neither the presence of God in our lives, nor the knowledge of His ways, we learned to live independently of God. During the early and formative years of our lives we developed mental strongholds or flesh patterns ("old nature" NIV). Some of those flesh patterns are defense mechanisms we incorporated to protect us from physical, emotional, and spiritual abuse. We learned how to cope, survive, and succeed by relying on our own strengths and resources. We tried to make a name for ourselves by enhancing our appearance, performance, and social status.

The language we learned to speak, our worldview, and perception of reality were assimilated from the environment in which we were raised. Most of this assimilation came through prevailing experiences, including the homes we were raised in, the schools we went to, the friends we chose, the church we attended or didn't attend. Although education plays a role, our attitudes about life are more caught than taught. Children aren't formally taught the language of their parents until they attend school. They learn to speak by observing their parents and peers. They also pick up their preferences and prejudices. However, two children raised in the same environment will respond differently to their parents and teachers. Even at the earliest ages we make personal choices as to how we respond to our environment.

Mental strongholds are also formed through traumatic experiences such as a death in the home, the separation or divorce of parents, emotional, physical, and sexual abuse by others. Attitudes and beliefs about God, ourselves, and life in general are deeply embedded in our memory. At the time of trauma, we mentally process what is happening and formulate beliefs about ourselves, other people, and God, such as, *God doesn't love me; I'm no good; this is my fault; I can never trust anyone; all men are perverts; I have to be self-sufficient.* We adapt certain ways to defend ourselves such as lying, withdrawing, blaming, denying, or rationalizing our behavior. Many will hold on to their anger, which they falsely believe will protect them from further abuse. These mental pathways in the brain are like ruts in a road. The car just keeps following the same old worn path, and any attempt to steer out of them is met with resistance.

We cannot regain by human effort what was lost in Paradise: intimacy, security, acceptance, and significance. Despite our best efforts we remain bound to our past if we choose not to repent and believe the gospel. We are darkened in our understanding, because we are alienated from the life of God (Ephesians 4:18). Paul has some rather scathing words for those who won't repent in Titus 1:15-16: "To the pure all things are pure, but to those who are defiled and unbelieving nothing is pure, but both their mind and their conscience are defiled. They profess to know God, but by their deeds they deny Him, being detestable and disobedient and worthless for any good deed."

Apart from Christ, we have no choice but to live according to our old nature. Our natural life in the flesh is sinful and idolatrous at its core. It is sinful because the essence of sin is to live independently of God. It is idolatrous because it places something other than God at the center of our lives, which of course is ourselves, as the following story illustrates:

> I grew up with a rage-aholic father. There was constant tension, verbal abuse, and anger expressed freely throughout my childhood. Not only by my parents, but by me as well. I did not realize there was anything wrong with this type of lifestyle, because it was all that had been modeled to me by the adults in my life. I began to understand that being raised in a dysfunctional home I had developed wrong patterns of living. I had adapted to the anger and rage around me by forming my own dysfunctional coping mechanisms. I built strong walls of protection around myself. I had a tough countenance and hard exterior. I would only let "certain" people "in" and was very guarded around people, because it was very difficult for me to trust anyone. I discovered that my "safe" emotion was anger, so every emotion I experienced

was expressed in anger of some sort. I was also very co-dependent, insecure, and performance-oriented. I feared rejection and craved approval and affirmation. I was a perfectionist who feared failure and disappointment. All of these areas were manifestations of the internalized anger I experienced growing up.

Because the flesh is self-serving and self-protecting it is by nature self*ish*. A selfish person will inevitably have angry confrontations with another selfish person, because both want their own way. It is not the nature of a selfish person to consider the other person more important than themselves, but it is God's nature (Philippians 2:3-4), otherwise we would all be doomed. James 4:1-3 comments on the nature of selfishness:

> What is the source of quarrels and conflicts among you? Is not the source your pleasures that wage war in your members? You lust and do not have; so you commit murder. You are envious and cannot obtain; so you fight and quarrel. You do not have because you do not ask. You ask and do not receive, because you ask with wrong motives, so that you may spend it on your pleasures.

But there is good news. "From now on, therefore, we regard no one according to the flesh. Even though we once regarded Christ according to the flesh, we regard him thus no longer. Therefore, if anyone is in Christ, he is a new creation. The old has passed away; behold, the new has come. All this is from God, who through Christ reconciled us to himself and gave us the ministry of reconciliation" (2 Corinthians 5:16-18 ESV). We are no longer "in Adam"; we are alive "in Christ." We have been delivered from the domain of darkness and transferred to the kingdom of His beloved Son, in whom we have redemption, the forgiveness of sins (Colossians 1:13-14).

If all that is true, then how come we still struggle with the same old issues we did before we were born again? Because apart from Christ, we programmed our minds to live independently of God, and unlike a computer there is no "delete" button. That is why Paul wrote in Romans 12:2, "Do not conform to the pattern of this world, but be transformed by the renewing of your mind. Then you will be able to test and approve what God's will is—his good, pleasing and perfect will" (NIV). Sadly, as believers we can continue to be conformed to this world if we keep doing what we have always done.

If we want to experience freedom from our past and grow in Christ we have to reprogram our minds, but we also have to check for "viruses." Computer viruses are never accidental. They are inserted by disgruntled employees and computer hackers. In the same way, the father of lies seeks to introduce destructive heresies through his myriad of deceiving spirits. We must not be ignorant of his schemes (thoughts). That is why Paul uses warfare language when describing how to tear down mental strongholds in 2 Corinthians 10:3-5:

> Though we walk in the flesh, we do not war according to the flesh, for the weapons of our warfare are not of the flesh, but divinely powerful for the destruction of fortresses. We are destroying speculations and every lofty thing raised up against the knowledge of God, and we are taking every thought captive to the obedience of Christ.

Jesus said, "The time is fulfilled, and the kingdom of God is at hand; repent and believe the gospel" (Mark 1:15). To *repent* means to *change one's mind*. In the early church they would literally face the West and say, "I renounce you Satan, and all your works, and all your ways." Then they would face the East and make their profession of faith in Christ. Salvation is not addition. We didn't just add Jesus to our lives. We are transformed when we believe the truth that will set us free. If we continue to believe as we always have and simply add on a new belief, we haven't truly repented. We can't believe a lie and the truth at the same time and expect our lives to be stable. A double-minded person is unstable in all their ways. The two *Steps to Freedom in Christ* at the end of this chapter and the next will help you tear down those mental strongholds.

Unfortunately there is no instant way of renewing our minds. Paul admonishes us to let the peace of Christ rule in our hearts, and we do that by letting the word of Christ richly dwell within us (Colossians 3:15-16). Think of your mind as a pot of coffee. At one time it was clear water, but coffee was introduced very early in life. Your mind became dark and smelly. Then one day you decide to clean up your mind, and you were surprised that the battle only intensified. Then you noticed that beside you was a bowl of crystal clear ice labeled *Word of God*. You couldn't dump the whole bowl into your pot at once, but you could put one cube of ice in every day. The psalmist wrote, "How can a young man keep his way pure? By guarding it according to your word...I have stored up your word in my heart, that I might not sin against you" (Psalm 119:9,11 ESV).

If you kept putting one cube of ice in every day, the water in your pot would become clearer with every addition. If you did it long enough, you wouldn't taste, smell, or see the coffee even though it is still there. That process will work provided you are not putting in more coffee along with the ice. If you want to clear your mind of lustful thoughts you have to stop looking at pornography. Like a computer, if you put garbage in, you will get garbage out. If you continue listening to the rhetoric of the intolerant, the rebellious, the bigot, the arrogant, the scoffer, and the atheist you will struggle renewing your mind. "Do not be deceived: 'Bad company ruins good morals'" (1 Corinthians 15:33 ESV).

Breaking Bondages

I was conducting a Living Free in Christ conference in Birmingham, Alabama, when I first met Mike Quarles. He was a Southern gentleman at peace with himself, and I was surprised when I heard his story as we worked on a book together on overcoming addictive behavior. His father was a raging, abusive alcoholic and his mother was extremely overprotective. Here's a portion of his story:

> As a child, I didn't introduce myself by saying, "Hi, I'm Mike Quarles. I'm unaccepted, inadequate, insecure and guilty. Something is wrong with me." In the recesses of my soul, however, those feelings were there. Like everyone, I longed to have my basic needs of love, acceptance and approval met. I developed my own patterns in how to deal with life, solve my problems, become a successful person and meet my needs. I don't remember any love between my mom and dad. In the house they fought violently in an ongoing war. Scattered into the arguments were a few moments of peace and calmness. Several times my dad turned over the kitchen table, scattering food across our floor and breaking dishes. I could not bring my friends home to such a miserable situation. Using any excuse, I stayed away from home as much as possible. In some of my most vivid childhood memories, I remember lying in bed at night and listening to my mom and dad in one of their violent arguments. Once my dad chased everyone out of the house with a loaded shotgun. I lived in fear that one morning I would find one of my parents had killed the other one. Today as I look back, I'm convinced it's a miracle no one

died a violent death. My brother is two years younger
and my sister four years younger than I am. As children,
we responded to our home life in a predictable manner.
As the oldest, I learned to fight and rebel against our
alcoholic father and his abusive authority. My brother
became the people pleaser and did anything to placate
Dad. My sister learned to withdraw, hide and stay out of
the way. Of course, we adopted these same patterns for
dealing with stress in our adult lives.[1]

Mike chose alcohol as his means of coping and became an alcoholic until he discovered who he is in Christ. It has been our privilege to serve together helping people overcome addictive behavior.
If there are patterns of alcohol and drugs in your family or in your
own experience, there will be intense anger. There will also be sexual bondage in the vast majority of users and abusers, a problem that
usually goes untreated in chemical dependency programs. Breaking
that bondage is the key to recovery.

Romans 6:1-14 identifies the believer with Christ in His life,
death, burial, and resurrection. We learn from Paul that it isn't what
we do that determines who we are. Who we are determines what we
do. We are not identified by our flesh patterns. We are not alcoholics, addicts, co-dependents, or co-addicts. We are children of God.
Paul argues that since we are children of God, natural death and
sin have no mastery over us. "So you also must consider yourselves
dead to sin and alive to God in Christ Jesus" (Romans 6:11 ESV). We
consider it so, because it is so. Death is the end of sin's controlling
relationship to us, but not its existence. Sin is still here and appeal-
ing, but because we are alive in Christ, we don't have to yield to it.

"There is now no condemnation for those who are in Christ Jesus.
For the law of the Spirit of life has set you free in Christ Jesus from
the law of sin and death" (Romans 8:1-2). Paul uses the word *law* in

this passage for a reason. You can't do away with a natural law. The law of sin and death is still operative. Because of our sin we will all physically die, but we will continue to live spiritually. Paul said, "For to me, to live is Christ and to die is gain" (Philippians 1:21). When we die, we will be absent from our decaying bodies and present with the Lord in resurrected and unperishable bodies. We overcome the law of sin and death by a greater law, which is *the law of the Spirit of life in Christ Jesus*. In the same way, we can't fly by overcoming the law of gravity by human effort. However, because of the law of thermodynamics we can fly "in" an airplane, which has the power to overcome the law of gravity.

Jesus died once for all our sins (Romans 6:10). When He did that all our sins were future. Any sin we commit tomorrow is already forgiven. There will be no more sacrifices for sin. That is not a license to sin; it is a gracious means not to sin. Jesus did His part, now we have to do ours. When sin makes its appeal we choose to believe that we are alive in Christ and dead to sin. It has no authority over us. Since we are no longer under the law, Satan has no basis to accuse us. Thus there is now no condemnation for those who are in Christ Jesus. Even though we are forgiven there is still the danger of the entrapment of sin that Paul warns about in Romans 6:12-14:

> Let not sin therefore reign in your mortal body, to make you obey its passions. Do not present your members to sin as instruments for unrighteousness, but present yourselves to God as those who have been brought from death to life, and your members to God as instruments for righteousness. For sin will have no dominion over you, since you are not under law but grace (ESV).

The problem with addictive behavior is the inevitable use of our bodies as instruments of unrighteousness. There is no way that one can commit a sexual sin without doing that, and doing so allows sin to reign in our mortal bodies. Confessing sinful behavior does not deal with the entrapment of sin as Paul explains above and in 1 Corinthians 6:15-18:

> Do you not know that your bodies are members of Christ? Shall I then take the members of Christ and make them members of a prostitute? Never! Or do you not know that he who is joined to a prostitute becomes one body with her? For as it is written, "The two shall become one flesh." But he who is joined to the Lord becomes one spirit with him. Flee from sexual immorality. Every other sin a person commits is outside the body, but the sexually immoral person sins against his own body (ESV).

In the Step at the end of this chapter you will be given the opportunity to pray and ask God to reveal to your mind every sexual use of your body as an instrument of unrighteousness. God will answer that prayer. He usually starts with your first experience and brings you to the present. Sadly, this includes incest and rape. Even though sexual abuse is against your will, the body is still defiled. We can't promise that won't happen in the future, but we can promise that you don't have to remain a victim forever. You can renounce that use of your body and ask God to break that *one flesh* bond spiritually, mentally, and emotionally. The presence and power of God has come to set you free from your past.

The way men have sexually treated women has fueled the anger of the feminist movement. Victims not only feel dirty and defiled, they are silently enraged by such violations. Silent, because they fear retribution if they speak up at home or work. Some are explosively angry and seek revenge.

If we want to be transformed by the renewing of our minds as instructed in Romans 12:2, then we must first follow the preceding verse: "I appeal to you therefore, brothers, by the mercies of God, to present your bodies as a living sacrifice, holy and acceptable to God, which is your spiritual worship" (12:1 esv) We can win the battle for our minds and be transformed when sin no longer wages war in our bodies.

Under the Old Testament Law, a sin offering was a blood-only sacrifice. The carcass was drained of blood and then disposed of outside the compound. "Without the shedding of blood there is no forgiveness of sins" (Hebrews 9:22 esv). Clearly our Lord and Savior Jesus Christ offered His blood for our sin, and His body was removed from the city. It is not enough, however, that our sins are forgiven. We would just be the same old person we were before, but forgiven. The burnt offering was a total sacrifice of the animal. The entire body was consumed in fire. *Burnt* in Hebrew literally means "that which ascends." We are urged to give our bodies to God as a burnt offering—a living sacrifice. Forgiveness removes the barrier, but we also must be filled with the Holy Spirit. Under the Law there was music 24 hours a day in the temple led by the Levitical priests. As a believer your body is a temple of God, and when you are filled with the Spirit the music begins, "addressing one another in psalms and hymns and spiritual songs, singing and making melody to the Lord with all your heart" (Ephesians 5:19 esv).

Discussion Questions

1. Why was there no anger in Paradise?

2. Adam and Eve went from acceptance, security, and significance to fear, depression, guilt, shame, and anger in a moment. The cause was sin, but what brought about the drastic change? What was different about

Adam and Eve the day before and the day after the
fall? What is the ultimate answer for all the anger, fear,
anxiety, and depression?

3. What is a mental stronghold or flesh pattern?

4. How are flesh patterns formed? Why does everybody
have different flesh patterns?

5. As new creations in Christ, how can we still be bound to
the past? Does God fix our past, or does He set us free
from it? How?

6. What changes and what doesn't change when we are
born again?

7. How are we transformed?

8. What is *repentance*?

9. How can we allow sin to reign in our mortal bodies?

10. How can we break the entrapment of sin?

Steps to Freedom in Christ

Bondage Versus Freedom

Many times we feel trapped in a vicious cycle of "sin, confess; sin,
confess" that never seems to end, but God's promises say, "God is
faithful, and he will not let you be tempted beyond your ability, but
with the temptation he will also provide the way of escape" (1 Corinthians 10:13 ESV), and "submit therefore to God. Resist the devil
and he will flee from you" (James 4:7). If you did not choose the way
of escape, and sinned, then you should confess that to God, ask Him
to fill you with His Holy Spirit, resist the devil by putting on the full
armor of God (see Ephesians 6:10-20), and he will flee from you.

Sin that has become a habit often may require help from a trusted brother or sister in Christ. James 5:16 says, "Confess your sins to one another, and pray for one another, so that you may be healed. The effective prayer of a righteous man can accomplish much." Sometimes the assurance of 1 John 1:9 is enough: "If we confess our sins, He is faithful and righteous to forgive us our sins and to cleanse us from all unrighteousness." Remember, confession is not saying, "I'm sorry." It is openly admitting, "I did it." Whether you need help from other people or just the accountability of walking in the light before God, pray the following prayer:

> *Dear Heavenly Father, You have told me to put on the Lord Jesus Christ and make no provision for the flesh in regard to its lust. I confess that I have given in to fleshly lusts that wage war against my soul. I thank You that in Christ my sins are already forgiven, but I have broken Your holy law and I have allowed sin to wage war in my body. I come to You now to confess and renounce these sins of the flesh so that I might be cleansed and set free from the bondage of sin. Please reveal to my mind all the sins of the flesh I have committed and the ways I have grieved the Holy Spirit. In Jesus's holy name, I pray. Amen.* (See Romans 6:12-13; 13:14; 2 Corinthians 4:2; James 4:1; 1 Peter 2:11; 5:8.)

The list on the next page contains many sins of the flesh, but a prayerful examination of Mark 7:20-23, Galatians 5:19-21, Ephesians 4:25-31, and other passages will help you to be even more thorough. Look over the list and ask the Holy Spirit to bring to your mind the sins you need to confess. He may reveal others to you as well. For each sin the Lord shows you, pray a prayer of confession from your heart. Use the sample prayer following the list to help you confess these sins to God.

Note: Sexual sins, marriage and divorce issues, gender identity, abortion, suicidal tendencies, perfectionism, eating disorders, substance abuse, gambling, and bigotry will be dealt with later in this Step.

__ Stealing	__ Quarreling/fighting	__ Jealousy/envy
__ Complaining/ criticism	__ Sarcasm	__ Gossip/slander
__ Swearing	__ Apathy/laziness	__ Lying
__ Hatred	__ Anger	__ Drunkenness
__ Cheating	__ Avoiding responsibility	__ Greed/ materialism

Others: _____

> *Dear Heavenly Father, I confess that I have sinned against You by (name the sins). Thank You for Your forgiveness and cleansing. I now turn away from these expressions of sin and turn to You, Lord. Fill me with Your Holy Spirit so that I will not carry out the desires of the flesh. In Jesus's name I pray. Amen.*

Resolving Sexual Sin

It is our responsibility not to allow sin to reign (rule) in our physical bodies. To avoid that, we must not use our bodies or another person's body as an instrument of unrighteousness (see Romans 6:12-13). Sexual immorality is not only a sin against God, but also a sin against your body, the temple of the Holy Spirit (1 Corinthians 6:18-19). Sex was intended by God to be the means for procreation and for the pleasure of a husband and wife. When marriage is consummated, they become one flesh. If we sexually join our bodies to another person outside of marriage we also become "one flesh" (1 Corinthians 6:16), which creates a spiritual bond between two people leading to spiritual bondage, whether it is heterosexual or homosexual. Sexual relations between people of the same sex are explicitly forbidden by God, but so is sex with someone of the opposite sex who is not your spouse. To find freedom from sexual bondage, begin by praying the following prayer:

> *Dear Heavenly Father, I have allowed sin to reign in my mortal body. I ask You to bring to my mind every sexual use of my body as an instrument of unrighteousness so that I can renounce these sexual sins and break those sinful bondages. In Jesus's name I pray. Amen.*

As the Lord brings to your mind every immoral sexual use of your body, whether it was done to you (rape, incest, sexual molestation) or willingly by you (pornography, masturbation, sexual immorality), renounce every experience as follows:

> *Dear Heavenly Father, I renounce (name the sexual experience) with (name). I ask You to break that sinful bond with (name) spiritually, physically, and emotionally. In Jesus's name I pray. Amen.*

If you have used pornography, say the following prayer:

> *Dear Heavenly Father, I confess that I have looked at sexually suggestive and pornographic material for the purpose of stimulating myself sexually. I have attempted to satisfy my lustful desires and polluted my body, soul, and spirit. Thank You for cleansing me and for Your forgiveness. I renounce any satanic bonds I have allowed in my life through the unrighteous use of my body and mind. Lord, I commit myself to destroy any objects in my possession that I have used for sexual stimulation and to turn away from all media that are associated with my sexual sin. I commit myself to the renewing of my mind and to think pure thoughts. Fill me with Your Holy Spirit that I may not carry out the desires of the flesh. In Jesus's name I pray. Amen.*

After you have finished, commit your body to God by praying:

Dear Heavenly Father, I renounce all these uses of my body as an instrument of unrighteousness, and I admit to any willful participation. I choose to present my physical body to You as an instrument of righteousness, a living and holy sacrifice, acceptable to You. I choose to reserve the sexual use of my body for marriage only. I reject the devil's lie that my body is not clean or that it is dirty or in any way unacceptable to You as a result of my past sexual experiences. Lord, thank You that You have cleansed and forgiven me and that You love and accept me just the way I am. Therefore, I choose now to accept myself and my body as clean in Your eyes. In Jesus's name I pray. Amen.

Special Prayers and Decisions for Specific Situations

The following prayers will enhance your growth process and help you make critical decisions. On their own they are unlikely to bring complete resolution or recovery, but they are an excellent starting point. You will then need to work on renewing your mind. Please don't hesitate to seek godly counsel for additional help when needed.

Marriage

Dear Heavenly Father, I choose to believe that You created us male and female, and that marriage is a spiritual bond between one man and one woman who become one in Christ. I believe that bond can only be broken by death, adultery, or desertion by an unbelieving spouse. I choose to stay committed to my vows and to remain faithful to my spouse until physical death separates us. Give me the grace to be the spouse You created me to be, and enable me to love and respect my partner in marriage. I will seek to change only myself and accept my spouse as You have accepted me.

Teach me how to speak the truth in love, to be merciful as You have been merciful to me, and to forgive as You have forgiven me. In Jesus's name I pray. Amen.

Divorce

Dear Heavenly Father, I have not been the spouse You created me to be, and I deeply regret that my marriage has failed. I choose to believe that You still love and accept me. I choose to believe that I am still Your child, and that Your desire for me is that I continue serving You and others in Your kingdom. Give me the grace to overcome the disappointment and the emotional scars that I carry, and I ask the same for my ex-spouse. I choose to forgive my ex-spouse, and I choose to forgive myself for all the ways I contributed to the divorce. Enable me to learn from my mistakes and guide me so that I don't repeat the same old flesh patterns. I choose to believe the truth that I am still accepted, secure, and significant in Christ. Please guide me to healthy relationships in Your church, and keep me from seeking a marriage on the rebound. I trust You to supply all my needs in the future, and I commit myself to following You. In Jesus's name I pray. Amen.

Gender Identity

Dear Heavenly Father, I choose to believe that You have created Your children to be male and female and commanded us to maintain a distinction between the two genders (Deuteronomy 22:5; Romans 1:24-29). As a new creation in Christ I choose to believe that I am a child of God and that You no longer regard me or any of Your children according to the flesh (2 Corinthians 5:16). I confess that I have judged others according to their flesh patterns. I pray that You will grant me the grace and wisdom to love and accept others, but not to condone either my sexual behavior or that of others that is clearly forbidden by Your Word. I choose to believe that my flesh patterns do not define who I am, or who any of Your children are. I confess that I have struggled with my own gender identity, and by faith, I choose to believe that You created me to be (a man / a woman). I stand against and renounce all the accusations and lies of Satan that would seek to convince me that I am somebody other than who You created me to be. Please enable me to overcome all sexual temptations, and enable me to crucify my flesh patterns. In the wonderful name of Jesus I pray. Amen.

Abortion

Dear Heavenly Father, I confess that I was not a proper guardian and keeper of the life You entrusted to me, and I confess that I have sinned. Thank You that because of Your forgiveness, I can forgive myself. I commit my child to You for all eternity and believe that he or she is in Your caring hands. In Jesus's name I pray. Amen.

Suicidal Tendencies

Dear Heavenly Father, I renounce all suicidal thoughts and any attempts I've made to take my own life or in any way injure myself. I renounce the lie that life is hopeless and that I can find peace and freedom by taking my own life. Satan is a thief and comes to steal, kill, and destroy. I choose to remain alive in Christ who said He came to give me life and give it abundantly. Thank You for Your forgiveness that allows me to forgive myself. I choose to believe that there is always hope in Christ and that my Heavenly Father loves me. In Jesus's name, I pray. Amen.

Drivenness and Perfectionism

Dear Heavenly Father, I renounce the lie that my sense of worth is dependent upon my ability to perform. I announce the truth that my identity and sense of worth are found in who I am as Your child. I renounce seeking the approval and acceptance of other people for my affirmation, and I choose to believe the truth that I am already approved and accepted in Christ because of His death and resurrection for me. I choose to believe the truth that I have been saved, not by deeds done in righteousness, but according to Your mercy. I choose to believe that I am no longer under the curse of the law, because Christ became a curse for me. I receive the free gift of life in Christ and choose to abide in Him. I renounce striving for perfection by living under the law. By Your grace, Heavenly Father, I choose from this day forward to walk by faith in the power of Your Holy Spirit according to what You have said is true. In Jesus's name I pray. Amen.

Eating Disorders or Self-Mutilation

Dear Heavenly Father, I renounce the lie that my value as a person is dependent upon my appearance or performance. I renounce cutting or abusing myself, vomiting, using laxatives or starving myself as a means of being in control, altering my appearance, or trying to cleanse myself of evil. I announce that only the blood of the Lord Jesus Christ cleanses me from sin. I realize I have been bought with a price and my body, the temple of the Holy Spirit, belongs to God. Therefore, I choose to glorify God in my body. I renounce the lie that I am evil or that any part of my body is evil. Thank You that You accept me just the way I am in Christ. In Jesus's name I pray. Amen.

Substance Abuse

Dear Heavenly Father, I confess that I have misused substances (alcohol, tobacco, food, prescription or street drugs) for the purpose of pleasure, to escape reality, or to cope with difficult problems. I confess that I have abused my body and programmed my mind in harmful ways. I have quenched the Holy Spirit as well. Thank You for Your forgiveness. I renounce any satanic connection or influence in my life through my misuse of food or chemicals. I cast my anxieties onto Christ who loves me. I commit myself to yield no longer to substance abuse, but instead I choose to allow the Holy Spirit to direct and empower me. In Jesus's name I pray. Amen.

Gambling

Dear Heavenly Father, I confess that I have been a poor steward of the financial resources that have been in my possession. I have gambled away my future, chasing a false god. I have not been content with food and clothing, and the love of money has driven me to behave irrationally and sinfully. I renounce making provision for my flesh in regard to this lust. I commit myself to staying away from all gambling casinos, gambling websites, bookmakers, and lottery sales. I choose to believe that I am alive in Christ and dead to sin. Fill me with Your Holy Spirit so that I don't carry out the desires of the flesh. Show me the way of escape when I am tempted to return to my addictive behaviors. I stand against all of Satan's accusations, temptations, and deceptions by putting on the armor of God and standing firm in my faith. I choose to believe that You will meet all my needs according to Your riches in glory. In Jesus's name I pray. Amen.

Bigotry

*Dear Heavenly Father, You have created all humanity in
Your image. I confess that I have judged others by the color of
their skin, their national origin, their social or economic status, their cultural differences, and their sexual orientation.
I renounce racism, elitism, and sexism. I choose to believe
"there is neither Jew nor Greek, there is neither slave nor free
man, there is neither male nor female; for you are all one
in Christ" (Galatians 3:28). Please show me the roots of
my own bigotry that I may confess it and be cleansed from
such defilement. I pledge myself "to walk in a manner worthy of the calling to which I have been called, with humility
and gentleness, with patience, bearing with one another in
love, eager to maintain the unity of the Spirit in the bond of
peace" (Ephesians 4:1-3 ESV). In Jesus's name I pray. Amen.*

CHAPTER SIX

FLESH PATTERNS

Once again [Paul] makes flesh stand for evil deeds. He does not mean that they destroyed their flesh; otherwise how were they going to live? For the crucified person is dead and inactive. But what he means is strict discipleship. Even if desires press hard they rage in vain. Since the power of the Spirit is such, let us live according to it, and let us be content with it.

Chrysostom, *Homily on Galatians* 5:24 (c. 395)

Evangelist D.L. Moody, the "Billy Graham" of the nineteenth century, had a sharp temper which he learned to control—usually. One evening, Moody was conducting two evangelistic services back to back. After the first service, as Mr. Moody was standing near the door welcoming the new crowd, a man approached him and delivered a highly offensive insult of some sort. Moody never later repeated it, but it must have been contemptible for in a sudden fit of anger, Moody shoved the man and sent him tumbling down a short flight of steps.

The man was not badly harmed, but Moody's friends wondered how he could possibly preach the second service. "When I saw Moody give way to his temper," said an observer, "I said to myself, 'The meeting is killed. The large number who have seen the whole thing will hardly be in condition to be influenced by anything more Mr. Moody can say tonight.'"

Moody called the meeting to order, stood, and with trembling voice spoke these words: "Friends, before beginning tonight I want to confess that I yielded just now to my temper, out in the hall, and have done wrong. Just as I was coming in here tonight, I lost my temper with a man, and I want to confess my wrong before you all, and if that man is present here whom I thrust away from me in anger, I want to ask his forgiveness and God's. Let us pray." Instead of a lost cause, the meeting seemed unusually touched that night, with many people deeply and eternally impressed with the gospel.[1]

Everyone has angry flesh patterns. It's the way we learned to live apart from Christ. "Those who belong to Christ Jesus have crucified the flesh with its passions and desires. If we live by the Spirit, let us walk by the Spirit" (Galatians 5:24-25). To be a fruitful disciple we have to live by faith in power of the Spirit. Flesh patterns are formed by false beliefs developed as a means of coping with life apart from Christ. In order to repent, one has to know what those false beliefs are, choose to renounce the lies, and believe the truth. The Step at the end of this chapter will help you do that in a broader sense. The content of this chapter will identify several angry flesh patterns and give you the opportunity to repent and turn away from them. Keep in mind that flesh patterns do not define who you are. You are children of God who are learning to be angry but not sin.

The Anger Avoider

Ron and Pat Potter-Efron identify those who suppress their anger as the *anger avoider*:

> Anger avoiders don't like anger much. Some avoiders are afraid of their anger, or the anger of others. Anger seems too scary to touch. They're scared of losing control if they get mad, of letting out the monster inside of them. Other avoiders think that it's bad to be angry. They've

learned sayings like, "Only dogs get mad" and "Be nice, don't be angry." They hide from their anger because they want to be liked.[2]

People who suppress their anger try to keep the peace at all costs. They want to be known as "nice" people. They feel very uncomfortable around anger and will accommodate and appease whenever possible. When that's not possible, they will withdraw. It is possible to be so well conditioned to avoiding and suppressing anger that one genuinely believes he or she simply has no anger. Such was the case with a dear friend of ours, who wrote:

> After my wife passed away and while in counseling, I was asked the question: "How much anger did you have?" I answered, "None." "You don't have any anger?" was the next question. "No, I don't have any anger," was my reply. "Well, how did it make you feel?" "I felt hurt, but I didn't have any anger!" They immediately went on to explain that if I felt hurt, then I had anger. They explained that when one feels hurt, they have anger. But I kept insisting on the fact that, "No, I don't feel angry." Then they changed their questions to: "Do you ever lose your temper?" "No!" "How do you feel about others getting angry and losing their temper?" I said, "I don't appreciate it." "How do you feel about Christians getting angry?" I replied, "I don't believe they should!" After some time they explained to me that I was stuffing my anger. I had it, but was just not acknowledging it. They pointed out that since I didn't believe in Christians being angry, I just kept denying mine and suppressing it; and that's why I didn't feel it. I really didn't believe that I had anger.

This man, who had served as a pastor for decades, finally understood how far out of touch with his emotions he had become. In a fleshly effort to stay in control, he had slammed the door shut on his emotional life. He believed the lie that he had to be in control and had himself become controlled. He was in bondage to his own emotional denial. After discovering his identity and freedom in Christ he wrote:

> Since I have acknowledged my emotions and have allowed myself to accept how I feel, I am enjoying so many good feelings of joy. I have come to see that when I stuffed my bad feelings I also stuffed my good ones. It's so freeing to be myself and experience the joy of walking in who I am in Christ—that I can have normal emotions, just like Jesus did when He lived upon earth.

Have you felt guilty when you experienced even a twinge of anger? Have you believed that good Christians don't get angry? Have you been angry with yourself for not being assertive enough? In the past, have you hung up the phone and kicked yourself internally for pledging money for a cause you really had no interest in supporting? Have you beat yourself up inside for letting a more powerful personality persuade you to take on another task that you knew you have neither the time nor energy to tackle? Realize that anger avoidance is a fleshly means of coping with the fear of anger, confrontation, disapproval, and rejection.

We cannot be right with God and not be real. God may have to make us real in order for us to be right with Him. That is called brokenness, which almost always brings emotional freedom. If you identify with the "anger avoider" we encourage you to say the following out loud:

> *I renounce the lie that I have to deny my emotions in order to have self-control. I announce the truth that I am free in Christ to be a real and authentic child of God who*

experiences the full range of emotions under the liberating power of God. I give myself permission to be angry when appropriate, but not sin.

We have seen extreme cases in which ritual abuse victims have been unable to express any emotions, including anger. These "zero effect" persons have been programmed to believe that if they express how they feel (cry, get angry) they or someone else will be hurt. Many are unable to shed a tear. We have seen tears immediately start to flow in ritual abuse victims after saying: *I renounce the lie that my crying or showing any emotion at all will cause harm or death to me or anyone else.*

The Anger Exploder

At the other end of the anger spectrum are the *anger exploders,* illustrated by the following testimony:

> I am currently working through the Freedom in Christ discipleship course with my pastor in a church congregational setting. Weekly I feel the bondage being broken and freedom settling in. I have always been a little bullheaded and am tempted to anger easily. My anger usually comes suddenly...and fiercely...scaring even myself at times. Usually it is stress-oriented and a culmination of events that I hold within me until that last little insignificant incident lights the very short fuse. When the smoke clears I am left feeling desolate and humiliated. I have tried desperately for years to control this anger but at best have only learned to avoid stressful situations and even that is not great. I would be so happy to be truly free from these fits of rage once and for all. I would love to know how to deal with anger the way Christ would have me to. It really wrecks my witness when I have rantings and I end up tearful before the Lord when they

do come. Please help me…I would truly love to be free
from anger.

Those who have a tendency to explode are like dormant volcanoes. There is always the threat of an eruption. If they had a seismograph attached to their emotions, they would find continual tremors taking place. They live in a constant state of agitation. Whereas calm people will normally be at a 0 or 1 on the anger scale, anger exploders wake up in the morning registering 5. There is a subtle underlying anger all the time! That's why they erupt in anger at the slightest provocation.

In most cases such people have been severely wounded, and they explode when someone touches their wounds. That will be dealt with in the next chapter. This kind of anger outburst can also be situational. People who have been under extreme pressure have no emotional reserve. That is true for all of us. There are times when we can handle almost anything, and then there are times when the complaint of a child can set off an overstressed parent. Mature people know their emotional limits and have learned to back away before the explosion.

Driven people are stress carriers. Their adrenal glands are pumping all the time. Years ago psychologist William Marston identified four behavioral styles into which he believed all people fall. John Geier and Dorothy Downey refined Marston's model and developed the *DiSC* test. This *DiSC* model identifies people as falling into one of the following four categories: dominant (D), influencing (i), steadiness (S), and compliance (C).[3]

In their book, *Understanding How Others Misunderstand You*, Ken Voges and Ron Braund define the dominant personality:

> Because of the High D person's concentration on tasks
> and goals, he has a tendency to be insensitive to the

feelings of others. Rarely is this deliberate neglect, but the intensity with which he strives to meet his objectives can cause him to consider emotional expressions as obstacles. The High D person is prone to see life as a battle during which any walls in his way must be torn down. Unfortunately, that approach is likely to result in emotional casualties along the way.[4]

High D's can become excellent leaders, like Joshua in the Bible who overcame great obstacles in possessing the Promised Land. With the right talent, they can become great athletes and coaches as well, being determined and strongly motivated by competition. But the same competitive fire that fueled a passionate Bill McCartney in the Spirit can also produce an angry Bobby Knight in the flesh. Bill McCartney left a successful football coaching career at the University of Colorado to found the Promise Keepers, a Christian ministry for men. Bobby Knight was fired from a "successful" basketball coaching career at Indiana University because he could not control his explosive temper.

Those who score high on the dominant scale are usually Type A personalities and task-oriented leaders who are highly motivated to accomplish their goals. The apostle Paul would probably fit into this category before his conversion. Paul describes his own drivenness in Acts 26:9-11:

> So then, I thought to myself that I had to do many things hostile to the name of Jesus of Nazareth. And this is just what I did in Jerusalem; not only did I lock up many of the saints in prisons, having received authority from the chief priests, but also when they were being put to death I cast my vote against them. And as I punished them often in all the synagogues, I tried to force them to blaspheme; and being furiously enraged at them, I kept pursuing them even to foreign cities.

Anger exploders must admit that being competitive, determined, goal-setters does not give them license to angrily control or trample people in the process. We are "created in Christ Jesus for good works" (Ephesians 2:10), so He expects us to accomplish something, but never at the expense of other people. God's Word admonishes the impatient person in James 1:19-20: "My dear brothers and sisters, take note of this: Everyone should be quick to listen, slow to speak and slow to become angry, because human anger does not produce the righteous life that God desires" (NIV).

A year after Shirley and I (Rich) were married, we moved to Manila, Philippines, to oversee a new ministry to high school students. Our first daunting task was to send follow-up material to over 52,000 students who had received Christ or indicated spiritual interest!

I immediately shifted from director into dictator. I drove myself, my wife, and my Filipino staff hard. I was impatient and insensitive, lashing out whenever they were unable or unwilling to perform up to my standards. I stepped on quite a few toes as I crusaded forward in my pursuit of finishing the follow-up task and establishing model ministries around the city.

One day I was reading in 1 Corinthians 13 and the Lord riveted my attention to verse 13, "But now abide faith, hope, love, these three; but the greatest of these is love." I sensed the Lord speaking to my mind and saying, "Rich, if someone were to look at your life, they would say you believed the greatest of these is faith."

Of course we are saved by faith, we walk by faith, and without faith it's impossible to please God. This illustration in no way diminishes faith's importance to the Christian life. But I knew what the Lord was saying. In an effort to reach my goals, I was using people to accomplish my goals instead of loving them. I had forgotten that the greatest of these is *love*. I broke down before the Lord, confessed my sin, and asked Him to make me a compassionate person.

Moses was the most humble man on earth (Numbers 12:3), and yet he was also a man given to angry outbursts. One day, he made a terrible mistake in his anger, as Numbers 20:7-12 records:

> The LORD spoke to Moses, saying, "Take the rod; and you and your brother Aaron assemble the congregation and speak to the rock before their eyes, that it may yield its water. You shall thus bring forth water for them out of the rock and let the congregation and their beasts drink." So Moses took the rod from before the LORD, just as He had commanded him; and Moses and Aaron gathered the assembly before the rock. And he said to them, "Listen now, you rebels; shall we bring forth water for you out of this rock?" Then Moses lifted up his hand and struck the rock twice with his rod; and water came forth abundantly, and the congregation and their beasts drank. But the LORD said to Moses and Aaron, "Because you have not believed Me, to treat Me as holy in the sight of the sons of Israel, therefore you shall not bring this assembly into the land which I have given them."

We believe there is a strong warning for dominant leaders in this passage. God is loving and kind and will take care of His people, even when human leaders fail. But if we trivialize the calling of God and try and control His people in anger, we may find the Lord rising up to oppose the very goals He once gave us. And we may only gaze with longing eyes upon the dreams we once strove so mightily to fulfill. If you identify with the "anger exploder," we encourage you to say out loud the following:

> *I confess my impatience and angry outbursts. I renounce the lie that my purpose in life is dependent upon the control or*

manipulation of other people. I choose to believe that nothing or no one can keep me from being the person God called me to be, and I choose to make no goal more important than loving God and loving people.

The Anger Addict

There is a surge of hormones into the blood when anger manifests. The adrenaline rush can be addictive. The Potter-Efrons explain the *anger addict*:

> Why, then, do some people seek [anger] out? How could anyone get hooked on anger? The answer is the rush. The anger rush is the strong physical sensation that comes with getting really mad. The rush is the result of the body's natural fight-or-flight response to danger. The surge of adrenaline. The faster heart rate. Quickened breathing. Tensed muscles. Anger activates the body. The adrenaline boost can help you feel strong. It injects excitement into a dull day.[5]

Like any addict, anger addicts build up a tolerance for the "drug." That means more intensity in order to get the same high. The result can be deadly—either on the road, in the home, or elsewhere. If you identify with the "anger addict," we encourage you to say out loud the following:

> *I confess and renounce seeking the rush of emotion and power that comes from unjustified and unrestrained anger. I choose to strive for self-control under the Lordship of Christ and the power of His Holy Spirit, and I choose to believe that the joy of the Lord is my strength.*

The Anger Exploiter

Closely akin to the anger addict is the *anger exploiter*. Angry exploiters bully people. By using their anger or the threat of anger, they seek to gain an advantage over other people. Others fearfully bow to their will. Some anger exploiters actually don't get angry at all. They just act angry or threaten anger, knowing others will submit to their beck and call. That is one of Satan's strategies. "Your adversary the devil prowls around like a roaring lion, seeking someone to devour" (1 Peter 5:8). Victims are consumed when lions roar paralyzing them in fear.

This flesh pattern is like a child's temper tantrum, which was learned from early childhood. Their parents responded to their child's rage by caving in to their demands. That stronghold is often entrenched in the preschool years but takes on a more sophisticated cloak as an adult. Some timid souls who have been pushed around all their lives discover one day that they can do that to others of lesser stature. That is called displaced anger, taking out our frustrations on innocent people.

Our (Rich and Shirley's) adopted son, Luke, came into our family at the tender age of four with a very advanced system of angry flesh patterns. Apparently, at the orphanage in Thailand where he lived, the "squeaky wheel got the oil." When we picked him up, we asked his caregiver through an interpreter what Luke did when he didn't get his way.

"He screams," she said with a smirk on her face.

That turned out to be the understatement of the century! In his early days in our home, any denial of his "wants" or any reprimand to his behavior sent him into a 45-minute fit. There was yelling, screaming, crying, throwing things, stomping his feet, you name it. Since his bedroom door opened out, I had to brace my feet against his door to keep him there for a few minutes of "time out." The door would literally bow outward as he put all his force against it to get out! At times his anger was pretty scary. Turn the clock ahead 20 or 30 years and imagine what Luke would be like were it not for consistent, loving discipline, and some very helpful medications.

If you identify with the "anger exploiter," we encourage you to say out loud the following:

> *I renounce using anger or the pretense of anger as a way of manipulating other people to my advantage. I choose to believe that motivating other people should come from love, acceptance, and affirmation rather than fear and intimidation.*

The Calculating Avenger

One of the most dangerous flesh patterns is the *calculating avenger*. This is a calculating, seething, and revengeful anger. They might say, "I don't get mad, I get even," but in reality they are smoldering with anger and hatred.

The Bible contains some graphic examples of this kind of flesh pattern. King David's son, Absalom, waited two full years after his brother, Amnon, had raped his sister, Tamar, to carry out his plan of revenge on him.

This simmering, festering anger showed up in Absalom again in plotting to overthrow the throne of David, who was his father. After three years in exile following his murder of Amnon, King David permitted Absalom to come back to Jerusalem to live. But David refused to see him for two more years, even though they lived minutes away from one another. This rankled Absalom to the bone.

Absalom secretly took revenge against David and stole the hearts of the people away from him (2 Samuel 15:6), conspiring to usurp his father's throne (2 Samuel 15:10). His vehement disdain for his father was further evidenced by Absalom sleeping with David's concubines (2 Samuel 16:22).

Esau, older twin brother of Jacob, became a calculating avenger in response to Jacob's deceitful theft of their father Isaac's blessing. Genesis 27:41 tells the story: "So Esau bore a grudge against Jacob because of the blessing with which his father had blessed him; and Esau said to himself, 'The days of mourning for my father are near; then I will kill my brother Jacob.'"

Fortunately for both brothers the story has a happy ending. Jacob escaped from Esau and the two were eventually reconciled years later. In the upcoming chapter on forgiveness, we will explain why taking revenge is wrong. For now let Romans 12:17-21 renew your mind to the truth:

> Never pay back evil for evil to anyone. Respect what is right in the sight of all men. If possible, so far as it depends on you, be at peace with all men. Never take your own revenge, beloved, but leave room for the wrath of God, for it is written, "Vengeance is Mine, I will repay," says the Lord. "But if your enemy is hungry, feed him, and if he is thirsty, give him a drink; for in so doing you will heap burning coals upon his head." Do not be overcome by evil, but overcome evil with good.

If you identify with the "calculating avenger" we encourage you to say out loud the following:

> *I renounce seeking revenge and allowing my anger to fester. I choose to let it go and let God be the judge and avenger. I choose to forgive others as God has forgiven me. I commit myself to growing in the grace and knowledge of my Lord and Savior Jesus Christ and to seeking to overcome evil with good.*

The Grump

Grumps may not be the scariest people to live with, but they have a most annoying flesh pattern. Like a persistent mosquito on a hot summer night, the grump is always buzzing around a listening ear with a truckload of complaints. Those with this flesh pattern are sad individuals. They choose to believe that life has dealt them a bad hand. They have allowed themselves to become victims of their circumstances. Whether they are disgruntled at God, others, themselves, or all of the above, they are angry people. They have never learned the value of always rejoicing, always praying, and always giving thanks (1 Thessalonians 5:16-18). Sometime in the past their hopes were demolished. They don't want to get their hopes up, because then they will never be disappointed.

You can live 40 days without food, seven days without water, seven minutes without air, but you can't really live a moment without hope. Hope is the present assurance of some future good as explained by Paul in Romans 5:1-5:

> Since we have been justified by faith, we have peace with God through our Lord Jesus Christ. Through Him we have also obtained access by faith into this grace in which we stand, and we rejoice in the hope of the glory of God. Not only that, we rejoice in our sufferings, know that suffering produces endurance, and endurance produces character, and character produces hope, and hope does not put us to shame, because God's love has been poured into our hearts through the Holy Spirit who has been given to us (ESV).

Ninety-five percent of the population is pessimistic by nature, because what we hear on the evening news is 95 percent bad. We have to read our Bibles to get the Good News and then talk to ourselves as the psalmist did: "Why are you cast down, O my soul, and why are you in turmoil within me? Hope in God; for I shall again praise him, my salvation and my God" (Psalm 42:5-6 ESV). We can curse the darkness or we can light a candle. If you identify with the "grump" we encourage you to say out loud the following:

> *I renounce my grouchy, angry, pessimistic, and hopeless out-look on life. I choose to believe that I serve a God of all hope. I choose to be thankful that I am forgiven, that I have new life in Christ who will meet all my needs according to His riches, and that He has prepared a place for me for all eternity.*

The Critical Perfectionist

The *critical perfectionist* struggles to live up to unrealistic expectations. They feel like a failure even though others are probably impressed with how much they accomplish and how well they do it! Those who believe they have to be perfect will have a lot of blocked goals, because they seek to control their environment and others in order to accomplish their objectives. Such was the case in the Bible for Martha who was ticked off at her sister for not helping to accomplish her objectives. So she asked Jesus to straighten out Mary. "But the Lord answered her, 'Martha, Martha, you are anxious and troubled about many things, but one thing is necessary. Mary has chosen the good portion, which will not be taken away from her'" (Luke 10:41-42 ESV).

Perfectionism is law-based living. Perfectionists set their standards high and then try their best to live up to them. When they can't, they feel like failures. They are motivated by the fear of failure. Grace-based Christians don't do what they do in order to be accepted. They are already accepted and that is why they do what they do. They don't labor in the vineyard hoping God will someday love them. God loves them and that is why they labor in the vineyard. Christianity can be separated from all other religions on the basis of one question. What does it take for you to be loved and accepted?

Once I was discipling a high school student whose father was critical and perfectionistic. Convinced that his boys couldn't really do anything right, one day he dared them to wash his truck. He promised them $25 when the job was done if he was unable to find a place they missed.

They should have known better. They worked hard trying to show their dad they could meet his high expectations. They couldn't (nobody could!) and with a smug sense of glee, he gave them no money. This was just one in a series of angry, demeaning events in the life of his eldest son, who one night tried to take his life via his Boy Scout knife. Fortunately, the restraining hand of God spared his life. Soon after, the redeeming grace of God saved his soul, though the residual effects of an angry, critical father continued to plague him.

If you identify with the "critical perfectionist" we encourage you to say the following out loud:

> *I renounce the lie that I have to perform in order to be loved and accepted. I renounce perfectionism and drivenness and the fear of being criticized and not measuring up. I choose to believe that God already loves and accepts me for who I am. Therefore I choose to accept myself, and others the way God has accepted me.*

The Passive Aggressive

Finally, there is *passive aggressive* anger defined by Les Carter and Frank Minirth:

Passive aggression is caused by a need to have control with the least amount of vulnerability. This form of anger is different from suppression in that the person knows he or she is angry (in contrast to suppressed anger, which is denied). But because this person assumes it is too risky to be open, he or she frustrates others by subtle sabotage. The need for control is evidence of a strong competitive spirit. Whereas healthy relationships do not keep score regarding right and wrong, the passive aggressive person is out to win. Like the openly aggressive person, the passive aggressive person is engaged in a battle for superiority. But this person has cleverly realized that too much honesty about personal differences lessens his or her ability to maintain an upper hand. In contrast, sly forms of handling anger tend to keep him or her in the driver's seat.[6]

There is an element of pride in controlling others by outwitting them, and God is opposed to the proud. This flesh pattern, like all others, will never humble itself. We have to choose to do that, believing that humility is confidence properly placed in the Lord Jesus Christ. Rather than trying to control others, why not walk in the light, speak the truth in love, and say something like, "I'm angry about this," and specify why.

The fear of confrontation and possible rejection drives passive aggressive people to do an "end around" rather than to take a direct approach to expressing their anger when relating to others. They stall and procrastinate rather than following orders. Passive aggression is a deceptive tactic that is more devilish than Christian. Peter wrote, "Do not repay evil for evil or reviling for reviling, but on the contrary, bless, for to this you were called, that you may obtain a blessing. For 'Whoever desires to love life and see good days, let

him keep his tongue from evil and his lips from speaking deceit'"
(1 Peter 3:9-10 ESV).

If you are prone to be "passively aggressive" when angry we
encourage you to say the following out loud:

> *I renounce using my anger to deceive, manipulate, and control others. I choose to walk in the light, speak the truth in love, and be angry, but not sin. I will seek to do unto others as I would have them do unto me.*

Discussion Questions

1. What should we learn from D.L. Moody's experience?

2. What are the false beliefs that drive the following flesh patterns and how can they be overcome?

   - The Anger Avoider
   - The Anger Exploder
   - The Anger Addict
   - The Anger Exploiter
   - The Calculating Avenger
   - The Grump
   - The Critical Perfectionist
   - The Passive Aggressive

3. How did each of your parents handle anger, and how has that affected you?

Steps to Freedom in Christ

Deception Versus Truth

The Christian life is lived by faith according to what God says is true. Jesus is the truth, the Holy Spirit is the Spirit of truth, God's Word is truth, and we are to speak the truth in love (see John 14:6; 16:13; 17:17; Ephesians 4:15). The biblical response to truth is faith regardless of whether we feel it is true or not. Christians are to forsake all lying, deceiving, stretching the truth, and anything else associated with falsehood. Believing lies will keep us in bondage. Choosing to believe the truth is what sets us free (John 8:32). David wrote, "Blessed [happy] is the man…in whose spirit there is no deceit" (Psalm 32:2 ESV). The liberated Christian is free to walk in the light and speak the truth in love. We can be honest and transparent before God, because we are already forgiven, and God already knows the thoughts and intentions of our hearts (Hebrews 4:12-13). So why not be honest and confess our sins? Confession means to agree with God. People in bondage are tired of living a lie. Because of God's great love and forgiveness, we can walk in the light and fellowship with God and others (see 1 John 1:7-9).

Begin this commitment to truth by praying the following prayer out loud. Don't let any opposing thoughts, such as *This is a waste of time* or *I wish I could believe this, but I can't*, keep you from pressing forward. God will strengthen you as you rely on Him.

Dear Heavenly Father, You are the truth, and I desire to live by faith according to Your truth. The truth will set me free, but in many ways I have been deceived by the father of lies, the philosophies of this fallen world, and I have deceived myself. I choose to walk in the light, knowing that You love and accept me just as I am. As I consider areas of possible deception, I invite the Spirit of truth to guide me into all truth. Please protect me from all deception as You "search me, O God, and know my heart; try me and know my anxious thoughts; and see if there be any hurtful way in me, and lead me in the everlasting way" (Psalm 139:23-24). In the name of Jesus I pray. Amen.

Prayerfully consider the lists in the three exercises over the next few pages, using the prayers at the end of each exercise in order to confess any ways you have given in to deception or wrongly defended yourself. You cannot instantly renew your mind, but the process will never get started without acknowledging your mental strongholds or defense mechanisms, also known as flesh patterns.

Ways You Can Be Deceived by the World

___ Believing that having an abundance of money and possessions will make me happy (Matthew 13:22; 1 Timothy 6:10)

___ Believing that eating food, drinking alcohol, or using drugs can relieve my stress and make me happy (Proverbs 23:19-21)

___ Believing that an attractive body, phony personality, or image will meet my needs for acceptance and significance (Proverbs 31:10; 1 Peter 3:3-4)

___ Believing that gratifying sexual lust will bring lasting satisfaction without any negative consequences (Ephesians 4:22; 1 Peter 2:11)

___ Believing that I can sin and suffer no negative consequences (Hebrews 3:12-13)

___ Believing that I need more than Jesus to meet my needs of acceptance, security, and significance (2 Corinthians 11:2-4;13-15)

___ Believing that I can do whatever I want regardless of others and still be free (Proverbs 16:18; Obadiah 3:1; 1 Peter 5:5)

___ Believing that people who refuse to receive Jesus will go to heaven anyway (1 Corinthians 6:9-11)

— Believing that I can associate with bad company and not become corrupted (1 Corinthians 15:33-34)

— Believing that I can read, see, or listen to anything and not be corrupted (Proverbs 4:23-27; Matthew 5:28)

— Believing that there are no earthly consequences for my sin (Galatians 6:7-8)

— Believing that I must gain the approval of certain people in order to be happy (Galatians 1:10)

— Believing that I must measure up to certain religious standards in order for God to accept me (Galatians 3:2-3; 5:1)

— Believing that there are many paths to God and Jesus is only one of the many ways (John 14:6)

— Believing that I must live up to worldly standards in order to feel good about myself (1 Peter 2:1-12)

Dear Heavenly Father, I confess that I have been deceived by (confess the items you checked above). I thank You for Your forgiveness, and I choose to believe Your Word and believe in Jesus, who is the truth. In Jesus's name I pray. Amen.

Ways to Deceive Yourself

— Hearing God's Word but not doing what it says (James 1:22)

— Saying I have no sin (1 John 1:8)

— Thinking I am something or someone I'm really not (Galatians 6:3)

— Thinking I am wise in this worldly age (1 Corinthians 3:18-19)

— Thinking I can be truly religious and not control what I say (James 1:26)

— Thinking that God is the source of my problems (Lamentations 3)

— Thinking I can live successfully without the help of anyone else (1 Corinthians 12:14-20)

Dear Heavenly Father, I confess that I have deceived myself by (confess the items checked above). Thank You for Your forgiveness. I commit myself to believe only Your truth. In Jesus's name I pray. Amen.

Ways to Wrongly Defend Yourself

___ Denial of reality (conscious or unconscious)

___ Fantasy (escaping reality by daydreaming, TV, movies, music, computer, or video games, drugs, alcohol)

___ Emotional insulation (withdrawing from people or keeping people at a distance to avoid rejection)

___ Regression (reverting back to less threatening times)

___ Displaced anger (taking out frustrations on innocent people)

___ Projection (attributing to another what you find unacceptable in yourself)

___ Rationalization (making excuses for your poor behavior)

___ Lying (protecting yourself through falsehoods)

___ Hypocrisy (presenting a false image)

Dear Heavenly Father, I confess that I have wrongly defended myself by (confess the items checked above). Thank You for Your forgiveness. I trust You to defend and protect me. In Jesus's name I pray. Amen.

The wrong ways we have employed to shield ourselves from pain and rejection are often deeply ingrained in our lives. You may need additional discipling or counseling to learn how to allow Jesus to be your rock, fortress, deliverer, and refuge (see Psalm 18:1-2). The more you learn how loving, powerful, and protective God is, the more you'll be likely to trust Him. The more you realize how much God unconditionally loves and accepts you, the more you'll be released to be open, honest, and (in a healthy way) vulnerable before God and others.

The New Age movement and postmodernism have twisted the concept of faith by teaching that we make something true by believing it. That is false. We cannot create reality with our minds; only God can do that. Our responsibility is to face reality and choose to believe what God says is true. True biblical faith, therefore, is choosing to believe and act upon what is true, because God has said it is true, and He is the truth. Faith is something you decide to do, not something you feel like doing. Believing something doesn't make it true; it's already true, therefore we choose to believe it! Truth is not conditioned by whether we choose to believe it or not.

Everybody lives by faith. The only difference between Christian faith and non-Christian faith is the object of our faith. If the object of our faith is not trustworthy or real, then no amount of believing will change that. That's why our faith must be grounded on the solid rock of God's perfect, unchanging character and the truth of His Word. For two thousand years Christians have known the importance of verbally and publicly declaring truth.

Read aloud the following Statements of Truth, and carefully consider what you are professing. You may find it helpful to read them aloud every day for at least six weeks, which will help renew your mind to the truth.

Statements of Truth

1. I recognize that there is only one true and living God who exists as the Father, Son, and Holy Spirit. He is worthy of all honor, praise, and glory as the One who made all things and holds all things together. (See Exodus 20:2-3; Colossians 1:16-17.)

2. I recognize that Jesus Christ is the Messiah, the Word who became flesh and dwelt among us. I believe that He came to destroy the works of the devil and that He disarmed the rulers and authorities and made a public display of them, having triumphed over them. (See John 1:1,14; Colossians 2:15; 1 John 3:8.)

3. I believe that God demonstrated His own love for me in that while I was still a sinner, Christ died for me. I believe that He has delivered me from the domain of darkness and transferred me to His kingdom, and in Him I have redemption, the forgiveness of sins. (See Romans 5:8; Colossians 1:13-14.)

4. I believe that I am now a child of God and that I am seated with Christ in the heavenly realms. I believe that I was saved by the grace of God through faith and that it was a gift and not a result of any works on my part. (See Ephesians 2:6,8-9; 1 John 3:1-3.)

5. I choose to be strong in the Lord and in the strength of His might. I put no confidence in the flesh, for the weapons of warfare are not of the flesh but are divinely powerful for the destruction of strongholds. I put on the full armor of God. I resolve to stand firm in my faith and resist the evil one. (See 2 Corinthians 10:4; Ephesians 6:10-20; Philippians 3:3.)

6. I believe that apart from Christ I can do nothing, so I declare my complete dependence on Him. I choose to abide in Christ in order to bear much fruit and glorify my Father. I announce to Satan that Jesus is my Lord. I reject any and all counterfeit gifts or works of Satan in my life. (See John 15:5,8; 1 Corinthians 12:3.)

7. I believe that the truth will set me free and that Jesus is the truth. If He sets me free, I will be free indeed. I recognize that walking in the light is the only path of true fellowship with God

and man. Therefore, I stand against all of Satan's deception by taking every thought captive in obedience to Christ. I declare that the Bible is the only authoritative standard for truth and life. (See John 8:32,36; 14:6; 2 Corinthians 10:5; 2 Timothy 3:15-17; 1 John 1:3-7.)

8. I choose to present my body to God as a living and holy sacrifice and the members of my body as instruments of righteousness. I choose to renew my mind by the living Word of God in order that I may prove that the will of God is good, acceptable, and perfect. I put off the old self with its evil practices and put on the new self. I declare myself to be a new creation in Christ. (See Romans 6:13; 12:1-2; 2 Corinthians 5:17; Colossians 3:9-10.)

9. By faith, I choose to be filled with the Spirit so that I can be guided into all truth. I choose to walk by the Spirit so that I will not carry out the desires of the flesh. (See John 16:13; Galatians 5:16; Ephesians 5:18.)

10. I renounce all selfish goals and choose the ultimate goal of love. I choose to obey the two greatest commandments: to love the Lord my God with all my heart, soul, mind, and strength and to love my neighbor as myself. (See Matthew 22:37-39; 1 Timothy 1:5.)

11. I believe that the Lord Jesus has all authority in heaven and on earth, and He is the head over all. I am complete in Him. I believe that Satan and his demons are subject to me in Christ since I am a member of Christ's body. Therefore, I obey the command to submit to God and resist the devil, and I command Satan in the name of Jesus Christ to leave my presence. (See Matthew 28:18; Ephesians 1:19-23; Colossians 2:10; James 4:7.)

CHAPTER SEVEN

HEALING ANGER WOUNDS

●

All this bitterness is not merely to be cleansed but to be "put away" altogether. Why should anyone try to contain it or hold it in? Why keep the beast of anger around so as to have to watch it constantly? It is possible to banish it, to expel it and drive it off to some mountain place.

Chrysostom (c. 395)

Charlotte Elliot of Brighton, England, was suffering from poor health that left her bitter toward God and life in general. A Swiss minister was having dinner with the Elliot family when Charlotte lost her temper and railed against God and family in a violent outburst. Her embarrassed family left the room, and the minister stared at her across the table. "You're tired of yourself, aren't you?" he said. "You're holding on to your hate and anger, because you have nothing else in the world to cling to. Consequently, you have become sour, bitter and resentful."

"What is your cure?" Charlotte asked. "The faith you are trying to despise," the minister said. As they talked, her heart softened and she asked, "If I wanted to become a Christian, what would I do?" He replied, "You would give yourself to God just as you are now, with your fightings and fears, hates and loves, pride and shame." "I would come to God just as I am? Is that right?" Charlotte asked.

Charlotte did come to Christ that night, and years later her brother, Rev. Henry Elliot, was raising funds for a school for the children of poor clergymen. To help her brother, Charlotte wrote the following poem based on John 6:37 "…the one who comes to Me I will by no means cast out" (NKJV).

> Just as I am, without one plea,
> But that Thy blood was shed for me,
> And that Thou bidst me come to Thee,
> O Lamb of God, I come! I come! [1]

This chapter is about making some of the hardest, but most life-transforming decisions of your life. Jesus came to set captives free and bind up the brokenhearted. Are you willing to let Jesus set you free from your past and heal your damaged emotions? We hope you have already made the biggest decision of your life to trust in Jesus for the forgiveness of your sins and to receive the gift of eternal life. If you have, then your soul is in union with God. Every believer is alive and free in Christ, but how many are living that way? All could if we let Him finish the good work He has begun in us.

We have previously discussed how to deal with our emotions by managing our thoughts and beliefs on a daily basis. But what about past traumas that have left us wounded, bitter, and discouraged? The critic may say, "All that was taken care of at the cross." In a sense that is true, but it is an incomplete statement. It is more accurate to say, "All that God had to do for us to be completely free from our past was accomplished at the cross and by the resurrection of Jesus." Now it is up to us to repent and believe the gospel. All that was pro-grammed into our minds in the past is still present in our memories. Deeply embedded lies from past traumas leave festering wounds and damaged emotions that are triggered by present events.

Have you ever discussed an issue with some acquaintances and suddenly someone gets angry and walks off in a huff? You probably wondered, "What did I say that caused that reaction?" You didn't know that person's history, but you obviously touched one of their hot buttons.

It is almost impossible to be emotionally neutral about anything. If I discussed sexual abuse in a church setting, the emotional response on a scale from one to ten would be from two to ten. It would be two if you have never been sexually abused and don't know anybody who has been, but you know it's wrong, so you have some feelings about it. If you had been recently abused sexually, you would be approaching ten right then just because we brought up the subject. Bring up the topic of racism or police brutality in a public setting and listen to the rhetoric. Strong feelings are evoked by the mere mention of the subjects. It would be positive feelings for those who have experienced the help and protection of the police, but negative feelings if you believed (rightly or wrongly) that you or your community are a victim of racial profiling.

Suppose you were terrorized by a neighborhood bully named Ralph when you were young. You haven't seen the brute in twenty years when a similar-looking stranger introduces himself by saying, "Hi, I'm Ralph." Flashback! You might think that such an experience would have no effect on you years later, but I doubt that you would name your first male child Ralph. A fellow seminary student years ago asked my forgiveness for the way he was responding to me. Actually, I hadn't noticed other than he didn't appear to be very friendly. He was aloof because I looked so much like his high school wrestling coach whom he despised. Seeing me triggered painful memories of high school.

Everybody has strong feelings about something. It is what we call a primary emotion developed in the past by good and bad experiences and established beliefs. There can be positive emotions triggered by present-day events. The smell of candles, the sounds of music, and the sight of home can usher in good memories. There are also smells, sights, and sounds that can trigger painful memories.

In a seminary class, I asked the students to share their home experience from ages eight to twelve. A female student who was sitting beside me became instantly angry, hit me on the shoulder and asked, "Why are you making us do this?" She was the classic adult child of an alcoholic father. Her way of dealing with those painful memories was to avoid talking about her family. That is how most people deal with negative primary emotions. They avoid anything that would trigger them. There are subjects they don't want to talk about, places they don't want to go, movies they can't watch, and people they avoid.

Your world can shut down if you have had a lot of trauma in your life. This is the basis for political correctness, which has run amuck. When you don't want to offend anyone, everyone eventually loses, because you can't have any civil discourse about critical issues that matter. Colleges are considering "safe zones," where nothing of substance is talked about. Coddling to their oversensitive spirits will not free them from their past nor prepare them for the future.

Two critical choices have to be made in order to set captives free and heal the wounds of the brokenhearted. First, we have to become a new creation in Christ. We are not just a product of our past. We are a product of Christ's work on the cross and His resurrection. God doesn't fix our past; He sets us free from it. In the past we processed events as natural people. Now because of our new identity and position in Christ we can reprocess them, but not as a victim.

A missionary couple was sent home from the field because of the wife's mental and emotional health. They were asked to make an appointment with me before they went home. It was my privilege to help her find her identity and freedom in Christ. Then they went to her parents' very dysfunctional home. While there, they discovered that her father was carrying on a homosexual affair. After a disastrous visit, they made an appointment to see me. "What should we do?" they asked. "We don't know if he has AIDS or even if mom knows about his affair." When they finished their story, I said, "Let's put this in perspective. First, aren't you glad that you discovered that about your father after you resolved your personal and spiritual conflicts this summer?" She said, "If I had gone straight home to that mess, I would not have been able to handle it." I continued, "Knowing that about your father, what does that do to your heritage?" She started to answer and then a smile broke out on her face, and she said, "Nothing! I'm a child of God."

After a conference, I spoke the following Sunday morning at the host church. At the end of the service, a 33-year-old lady was sitting alone and looking very defeated. She said, "I went to your conference, but I'm not free." I asked if she was married and she said angrily, "No, and I am never going to be!" She had recently become a Christian, so I suspected there was probably a lot of immorality in her past, and that was the case. I asked if she had dealt with those issues as she went through the Steps, and she thought she had. I asked her, "Is there one defining moment in your life that stands out from all others?" "Yes," she said. "That would be when I was five years old."

I asked her to close her eyes and recall as best as she could what had happened then. Her mother had just come home from the hospital with her third child. I said, "Picture in your mind the setting and tell me what you see." She saw her mom holding her younger brother, and her dad cursing and yelling as he walked out of their lives. As she recalled the memory, the tears began to flow, and I asked, "What were you thinking at the time?" She said, "I have to be strong. I can't trust men. I will never get married." "Who else do you see in your memory?" I asked. With closed eyes she said, "Jesus!" "What's He saying to you," I asked. "Nothing," she said. "He just has His arms outstretched to me." "Why don't you go to Him?" I said.

The lies she believed as a result of that traumatic experience guided this tough, attractive, professional lady for years. I encouraged her to renounce them, which she did. Then I said, "You have never had a real father. Can I be your father for a moment?" She shrugged in agreement, and I said, "As your father, I would want you to get up in the morning, look in the mirror, and like what you see. I would wish for you to have a husband who would love you for the rest of your life, and I would like you to bring me a grandchild that I could love as I love you." She had never had an adult male authority figure talk to her that way. It was a life-changing moment for her.

Second, to be free from our past we have to forgive as Christ has forgiven us. Forgiving their fathers was the major turning point in both the above stories. Whenever we are asked to help someone who has a root of bitterness, the source of their problem has always been unforgiveness. There is no issue bigger in Christendom than forgiveness. Without God's forgiveness we are hopelessly lost.

There are three Greek words translated "forgive" in the New Testament. Put together, these three words give us a powerful picture of what it means to forgive those who have offended us. The first word, *aphiemi*, means literally "to send away" and refers in Matthew 6:12 to "cancelling a debt" as a picture of forgiveness. The beauty of this word is that it not only denotes the removal of any punishment incurred by the debt (or sin) but also the complete eradication of the debt (or sin) itself. It is as if the offense never occurred. The application for us is that just as God has pardoned us from sin's penalty and will never hold our sins against us, so we should treat one another.

The second word, *charizomai* (found in Ephesians 4:32 as well as other places in Scripture), is related to the word *grace* and refers to the giving of a good gift that is completely undeserved and unearned. We did not deserve God's forgiveness, but still God gave it. Those who have hurt us likewise do not deserve to be forgiven, but we are called to be like God and grant the pardon freely anyway.

Finally, *apoluo* is only used once pertaining to forgiveness in the New Testament (Luke 6:37). The word literally means to release or set free. Combining these three words gives us a complete picture of forgiveness. To forgive another is to give that person an undeserved gift by canceling out their debt of sin that is owed to you, demanding nothing in payment, releasing that person, and setting the person completely free by not holding the offense against them anymore. This is exactly what God in Christ has done for us, and what He has instructed us to give to others (Colossians 3:13; Ephesians 4:32). Freely we have received, and freely we give.

In the middle of the Lord's Prayer we are instructed to ask our Heavenly Father to "forgive us our debts, as we have forgiven our debtors" (Matthew 6:12). Why is that? Because our relationship with God is inextricably bound up with others. "We love because he first loved us. If anyone says, 'I love God,' and hates his brother, he is a liar; for he who does not love his brother whom he has seen cannot love God whom he has not seen. And this commandment we have from him: whoever loves God must also love his brother" (1 John 4:19-21 ESV). That is humanly impossible without God's grace within us.

Previously we explained that *agape*, God's love, is not dependent upon the object. God is not asking us to "like" an abuser. Nobody can order their emotions to do that. He is asking us to relate to others as He has related to us, to do the right thing on their behalf whether we feel like it or not. That may include tough love, like turning them in to the police or exercising church discipline, which is a proof of our love. Doing the right thing does not negate the need to personally forgive the one you are confronting.

Peter asked Jesus, "'Lord, how often shall my brother sin against me and I forgive him? Up to seven times?' Jesus said to him, 'I do not say to you, up to seven times, but up to seventy times seven'" (Matthew 18:21-22). Then Jesus told a parable in verses 23-25 about a king who wished to settle accounts with his servants. One owed him ten thousand talents and he couldn't possibly pay such a debt, which was way beyond a lifetime of wages. So the king ordered him to be sold into slavery. The servant fell on his knees and begged for mercy promising to pay everything. Out of pity the master released him and forgave his debt.

Three words need to be defined before we finish the parable: justice, mercy, and grace. *Justice* is fairness or rightness. If we meted out justice we would be giving someone what they deserved. God is a righteous God and cannot be otherwise. If He gave us what we deserved, we would all go to hell. Justice had to be served, and that is why Jesus went to the cross. He took upon Himself the punishment we deserved. God is also *merciful.* "But when the goodness and loving kindness of God our Savior appeared, he saved us, not because of works done by us in righteousness, but according to his own mercy" (Titus 3:4-5 ESV). Mercy is not giving someone what they deserve. If we throw ourselves upon the mercy of the court we are saying, "I was wrong, but I am asking for leniency that you don't give me what I deserve." *Grace* is giving undeserving people what they need.

Everything good in life, and indeed life itself, originates from God. We love because He first loved us. We are to be merciful as He has been merciful to us. In other words, in mercy don't give people what they deserve, but don't stop there. Be gracious. Give them what they don't deserve. "Love your enemies, and do good, and lend, expecting nothing in return, and your reward will be great, and you will be sons of the Most High, for he is kind to the ungrateful and the evil. Be merciful, even as your Father is merciful" (Luke 6:35-36 ESV).

Back to the parable. The forgiven slave sought out a fellow slave who owed him a hundred denarii. A denarii is a day's wage, which is a very small amount compared to ten thousand talents. When he couldn't pay it, the ungrateful slave choked him and sent him to prison. The point that can't be missed is that the moral disparity between us and God is thousands of times greater than that which exists between us and the most offensive of people. Hard to fathom isn't it? Most of us probably think we are living a righteous life, at least in comparison to others. But therein lies the danger. We are comparing ourselves to others instead of God.

Such was the case for the Pharisees who were criticizing Jesus for letting a known "sinner" fawn all over Him, but Jesus had something to say to them. "Therefore I tell you, her sins, which are many, are forgiven—for she loved much. But he who is forgiven little, loves little" (Luke 7:47 ESV). How much have you been forgiven? Little? Or much? How we answer that question will affect our capacity to love.

In the parable, the master said, "'You wicked servant! I forgave you all that debt because you pleaded with me. And should not you have had mercy on your fellow servant, as I had mercy on you?' And in anger his master delivered him to the jailers, until he should pay all his debt. So also my heavenly Father will do to every one of you, if you do not forgive your brother from your heart" (Matthew 18:32-35 ESV). In some Bible translations the word "torturers" is used instead of "jailors." Jailors may have tormented the inmates, but that misses the spiritual connotation of the word. The same root word was used by demons who accused Jesus of tormenting them (Mark 5:7), the eternal torment that will come upon those who worship the beast in Revelation 14:10, and upon Satan and his demons (20:10). Paul urged the church in Corinth to forgive someone "so that we would not be outwitted by Satan; for we are not ignorant of his *designs* [*noema*, i.e., thoughts]" (2 Corinthians 2:11 ESV, emphasis added). Unforgiveness has probably afforded Satan more access to the church than any other open door. Bitter people struggle with tormenting thoughts when they lie awake at night thinking of how others have hurt them.

God doesn't turn us over to the tormentors to inflict more pain on us. This is a disciplinary move convicting us to forgive others as He has forgiven us. He doesn't want the sun to go down on our wrath, so He prompts us to face the issue. "See to it that no one fails to obtain the grace of God; that no 'root of bitterness' springs up and causes trouble, and by it many become defiled" (Hebrews 12:15 ESV). We try to push down the painful memories, but God is trying to surface them so we can let them go. Forgiveness is to set a captive free and then realize that we were the captives. Without forgiveness we are bound to the past.

Forgiveness is not forgetting. When the Lord says that He will remember our sins no more (Isaiah 43:25), He is not saying that He will forget them. God couldn't forget anything even if He wanted to, because God is omniscient. It means that He will not take the past and use it against us in the future. "As far as the east is from the west, so far does he remove our transgressions from us" (Psalm 103:12 ESV). When we say to others, "Two years ago you did…," we are actually saying, "I haven't forgiven you." There will be no harmony in our homes and churches if we keep digging up the past and using it against each other. That doesn't mean that we don't testify in a court of law to ensure social justice. We should do that, but for our sakes we should forgive that person before we testify.

God forgives, but He doesn't tolerate sin, and neither should we.

We will never help an abuser by allowing them to continue in their sin. The abused have every right to set up scriptural boundaries to stop further abuse. If the abuser won't repent when confronted, we should report them to civil authorities. There are laws in the land against domestic and workplace violence, against verbal, physical, spiritual, and sexual abuse. We are fully aware of the risks involved in being a whistle-blower at home or work. We suggest legal counsel if that be the case.

After speaking on forgiveness, an angry lady approached me and said, "Sure, I'm supposed to just forgive them for ruining my life. Ten years ago my best friend walked off with my husband." "That is tragic," I said. "I'm so sorry that happened to you, but you need to let that go." "But you don't know how bad they hurt me," she said. "They're still hurting you," I replied. "Staying angry at them is only hurting yourself. It is like swallowing poison hoping the other person will die. I see a wounded lady with one arm in the air, because God has a firm grip on you and won't let go. Your other arm is hanging straight down, because you are holding on to the past with all your strength. Why don't you let go of the past, and grab hold of God with both hands?" "I'll think about it," she said. She went through the Steps later that day, and the change was so dramatic that her pastor's wife wondered what happened to her when she saw her Sunday morning. Whoever wrote the following said it well:

> Once I held in my tightly clenched fist...ashes. Ashes from a burn inflicted upon my 10-year-old body. Ashes I didn't ask for. The scar was forced on me. And for 17 years the fire smoldered. I kept my fist closed in secret, hating those ashes, yet unwilling to release them. Not sure if I could. Not convinced it was worth it. Marring the things I touched and leaving black marks everywhere...or so it seemed. I tried to undo it all, but the

marks were always there to remind me that I couldn't. I really couldn't. But God could! His sweet Holy Spirit spoke to my heart one night in tearful desperation. He whispered, "I want to give you beauty for your ashes, the oil of joy for your mourning and the garment of praise for your spirit of heaviness." I had never heard of such a trade as this: Beauty? Beauty for ashes? My sadly stained memory for His healing Word? My soot-like dreams for His songs in the night? My helpless and hurting emotions for His ever-constant peace?

How could I be so stubborn as to refuse an offer such as this? So willingly, yet in slow motion, and yes, while sobbing, I opened my bent fingers and let the ashes drop to the ground. In silence, I heard the wind blow them away. Away from me…forever. I am now able to place my open hands gently around the fist of another hurting soul and say with confidence, "Let them go. There really is beauty beyond your comprehension. Go ahead—trust Him. His beauty for your ashes."[2]

I was being interviewed on a Christian television network on the topic of sexual abuse. We were coming to the end of our time when the host asked me to close by praying for those who have suffered such an indignity. I said, "Before I do that I need to say something. In the majority of cases the abusers will never come back and say they are sorry or own up to their sin, and that leaves you struggling for closure. You hesitate to forgive, because you at least want some admission of sin. Ladies, since they won't come back, may I? As a man, a husband, and a father, would you forgive us men for the way we looked at you, touched you, and raped you? That is not your fault. That is our sickness. For your sake, please forgive us." Then I prayed for them and we went off the air. It was a good thing we did, because the host was sobbing uncontrollably.

Many hesitate to forgive others, because they wrongly think they have to do that in person. Our need to forgive others is initially only an issue between ourselves and God. The only time you should forgive another person in their presence is when they ask for it in your presence. In almost all other cases it is unadvisable to go to them, which could only set you up for more abuse. Sometimes people don't even know that they offended you, and telling them that you forgive them only creates a new problem. Besides, the person or people you may need to forgive could have died a long time ago, but their death didn't do anything to resolve your bitterness or heal your wounds. Moving away from abusers won't help either, because the problem is within ourselves. If you have offended someone else, then you need to go to them, but if you have been hurt by someone else you only need to go to God. What is to be gained is your own freedom. You don't forgive another person for their sake. You do it for your sake, and for your own relationship with God. That is why we see people set free in our offices as they work through the painful process of forgiving others. Your freedom is not dependent upon anyone else. If you are refusing to forgive another until they ask for it, every sick person in the world can hold you hostage by refusing to admit their fault or ask for your forgiveness.

"But why should I let them off my hook?" cry the wounded. That is exactly why you should, because if you don't you are still hooked to them and still bound to your past. If you let them off your hook, they are not off God's hook. "If possible, so far as it depends on you, live peaceably with all. Beloved, never avenge yourselves, but leave it to the wrath of God, for it is written, 'Vengeance is mine, I will repay says the Lord'" (Romans 12:18-19 ESV).

Natural people want to get even, to have the other person suffer as they have suffered. That is a flesh pattern and so is the twisted satisfaction of hating the wretch. It only puts you on the same moral plane as the offender. Would getting even heal your wounds or set you free? Would it resolve your anger problem? Where then is the justice? It's on the cross that justice was satisfied. Jesus died for your sins, his sins, her sins, all our sins. Forgiveness without the cross is morally offensive. We will never have perfect justice in this lifetime, but we will in eternity. We have to trust God that He will make everything right in the end. Every person will stand before the judgment seat of Christ and give an account of their life. Choose freedom, get on with your life, and let God deal with that person.

We are to forgive as God in Christ has forgiven us (Ephesians 4:32). How did Christ do that? He took the consequences of our sins upon Himself. When we forgive others we are agreeing to live with the consequences of their sins. "But that isn't fair," cry the victims. They're right. It isn't fair, but they will have to anyway. We are all living with the consequences of other people's sins. In fact every descendent of Adam and Eve is living with the consequences of Adam's sin. The only real choice we have living in this fallen world is to remain in the bondage of bitterness or choose the freedom of forgiveness. Forgiveness is a crisis of the will. For your sake, choose forgiveness.

I was doing a conference in California, which was cohosted by Link Care, a wonderful ministry that serves missionaries. A first-term couple was sent there straight from the mission field. The wife especially was angry and badly wounded by the other missionaries and had no intention of ever going back. All Link Care clients were encouraged to attend the conference, which was held at a local church. I couldn't help but notice her on Sunday evening. She never sang as she sat there with a scowl on her face. Monday afternoon I met with them at Link Care, and I asked them to introduce themselves. The wife was the last to respond and she said, "Frankly, I hate you." "Why is that?" I asked. She said, "I just want to go home, and because of you I have to stay another week." I told her that I would really like to hear her story, and she agreed to share it with me.

She had every right to be angry, and after hearing her story I asked if she would like to resolve her personal and spiritual conflicts. She agreed and I took her through the Steps. When she came to the Step on forgiveness, she prayed and made a list of who she needed to forgive. I explained to her what that decision really is and how to do it. She stared at the names on the list and pushed the paper away. I waited. She pulled the list back and then pushed it away again. Finally, after several minutes, she said, "My counselor has been trying to get me to cry ever since I came here." I had not mentioned the word to her. Finally she pulled the list back and began with the first name. "Lord, I forgive...," then the dam broke, and tears freely flowed. That night she was singing in church for the first time in months, and the anger that defined her on the first evening was gone.

To forgive from the heart we have to acknowledge the hurt and the hate. It is human nature to want to suppress such feelings, but they must be allowed to surface. That is the only way we can let them go. To help inquirers do that, we encourage them to say, "Lord, I forgive (name) for (whatever painful memory comes to their mind), because it made me feel (dirty, unloved, rejected, demeaned, worthless, etc.)." We encourage them to stay with each person on the list until they have dealt with everything that has caused them pain before moving on to the next person. If you just say, "I forgive my dad" and quickly move to the next person on the list, nothing happens. It is in the "what for" that makes it real. The Step at the end of this chapter provides more teaching on forgiveness and will help you identify who you need to forgive as you go through the process. It is your decision. We pray that you don't miss this moment of grace.

Discussion Questions

1. What are some of the reasons that people resist the gracious work of God?

2. What is a primary emotion and how is it triggered?

3. What triggers positive and negative emotions in you, and what is the origin of those feelings?

4. How are primary emotions healed?

5. Why is the need to forgive others so central to our Christian message?

6. What is the difference between justice, mercy, and grace?

7. Can we have a righteous relationship with God separate from how we relate to others? Explain.

8. What is forgiveness, i.e., if you forgave someone, what would you be doing or not doing?

9. Why are some people hesitant to forgive others even though they know they need to?

10. How do you forgive from the heart?

Steps to Freedom in Christ

Bitterness Versus Forgiveness

We are called to be merciful just as our Heavenly Father is merciful (Luke 6:36) and to forgive others as we have been forgiven (Ephesians 4:31-32). Doing so sets us free from our past and doesn't allow Satan to take advantage of us (2 Corinthians 2:10-11). Ask God to bring to your mind the people you need to forgive by praying the following prayer aloud:

Dear Heavenly Father, I thank You for the riches of Your kindness, forbearance, and patience toward me, knowing that Your kindness has led me to repentance. I confess that I have not shown that same kindness and patience toward those who have hurt or offended me (Romans 2:4). Instead, I have held on to my anger, bitterness, and resentment toward them. Please bring to my mind all the people I need to forgive so I may now do so. In Jesus's name I pray. Amen.

On a separate sheet of paper, list the names of people who come to your mind. At this point don't question whether you need to forgive them or not. Often we hold things against ourselves as well, punishing ourselves for wrong choices we've made in the past. Write "myself " at the bottom of your list if you need to forgive yourself. Forgiving yourself is accepting the truth that God has already forgiven you in Christ. If God forgives you, you can forgive yourself!

Also write down "thoughts against God" at the bottom of your list. Obviously, God has never done anything wrong, so He doesn't need our forgiveness, but we need to let go of our disappointments with our Heavenly Father. People often harbor angry thoughts against Him because He did not do what they wanted Him to do. Those feelings of anger or resentment toward God need to be released. Before you begin working through the process of forgiving those on your list, review what forgiveness is and what it is not. The critical points are highlighted in bold print.

Forgiveness is not forgetting. People who want to forget all that was done to them will find they cannot do it. When God says He will remember our sins no more, He is saying that He will not use the past against us. Forgetting is a long-term by-product of forgiveness, but it is never a means toward it. Don't put off forgiving those who have hurt you. Once you choose to forgive someone, then Christ will begin to heal your wounds. We don't heal in order to forgive; we forgive in order to heal.

Forgiveness is a choice, a decision of the will. Since God requires you to forgive, it is something you can do. Some people hold on to their anger as a means of protecting themselves against further abuse, but all they are doing is hurting themselves. Others want revenge. The Bible teaches, "'Vengeance is Mine, I will repay,' says the Lord" (Romans 12:19). Let God deal with the person. Let him or her off your hook because as long as you refuse to forgive someone, you are still hooked to that person. You are still chained to your past, bound up in your bitterness. By forgiving, you let the other person off your hook, but he or she is not off God's hook. You must trust that God will deal with the person justly and fairly, something you simply cannot do. "But you don't know how much this person hurt me!" you say. No other human really knows another person's pain, but Jesus does and instructs us to forgive others for our own sake. Until you let go of your bitterness and hate, the person is still hurting you. Nobody can fix your past, but you can be free from it. What you gain by forgiving is freedom from your past and freedom from those who have abused you. Forgiveness is to set a captive free and then realize you were the captive.

Forgiveness is agreeing to live with the consequences of another person's sin. We are all living with the consequences of someone else's sin. The only choice is to do so in the bondage of bitterness or in the freedom of forgiveness. But where is the justice? The cross makes forgiveness legally and morally right. Jesus died once for all our sins. We are to forgive as Christ has forgiven us. He did that by taking upon Himself the consequences of our sins. God "made Him who knew no sin to be sin on our behalf that we might become the righteousness of God in Him" (2 Corinthians 5:21). Do not wait for the other person to ask for your forgiveness. Remember, Jesus did not wait for those who were crucifying Him to apologize before He forgave them. Even while they mocked and jeered at Him, He prayed, "Father, forgive them; for they do not know what they are doing" (Luke 23:34).

Forgive from your heart. Allow God to bring to the surface the painful memories and acknowledge how you feel toward those who've hurt you. If your forgiveness doesn't touch the emotional core of your life, it will be incomplete. Too often we're afraid of the pain, so we bury our emotions deep down inside us. Let God bring them to the surface, so He can begin to heal those damaged emotions.

Forgiveness is choosing not to hold someone's sin against him or her anymore. It is common for bitter people to bring up past offenses with those who have hurt them. They want them to feel as bad as they do! But we must let go of the past and choose to reject any thought of revenge. This doesn't mean you continue to put up with the abuse. God does not tolerate sin and neither should you. You will need to set up scriptural boundaries that put a stop to further abuse. Take a stand against sin while continuing to exercise grace and forgiveness toward those who hurt you. If you need help setting scriptural boundaries to protect yourself from further abuse, talk to a trusted friend, counselor, or discipler.

Don't wait until you feel like forgiving. You will never get there. Make the hard choice to forgive even if you don't feel like it. Once you choose to forgive, Satan will lose his hold on you, and God will begin to heal your damaged emotions. Start with the first person on your list, and make the choice to forgive him or her for every painful memory that comes to your mind. Stay with that individual until you are sure you have dealt with all the remembered pain. Then work your way down the list in the same way. As you begin forgiving people, God may bring to your mind painful memories you've totally forgotten. Let Him do this even if it hurts. God is surfacing those painful memories so you can face them once for all time and let them go. Don't excuse the offender's behavior, even if it is someone you are really close to. Don't say, "Lord, please help me to forgive." He is already helping you and will be with you all the way through the process. Don't say, "Lord, I want to forgive," because that bypasses the hard choice we have to make. Say, "Lord, I choose to forgive these people and what they did to me." For every painful memory that God reveals for each person on your list, pray:

> *Dear Heavenly Father, I choose to forgive (name the person) for (what they did or failed to do), because it made me feel (share the painful feelings, i.e., rejected, dirty, worthless, inferior, etc.).*

After you have forgiven every person for every painful memory, then pray as follows:

> *Lord Jesus, I choose not to hold on to my resentment. I relinquish my right to seek revenge and ask You to heal my damaged emotions. Thank You for setting me free from the bondage of my bitterness. I now ask You to bless those who have hurt me. In Jesus's name I pray. Amen.*

Note: During this Step God may have brought to your mind people you have knowingly or unknowingly wounded. See below for instruction on how to seek the forgiveness of others.

Seeking the Forgiveness of Others

Jesus said, "So if you are offering your gift at the altar and there remember that your brother has something against you, leave your gift there before the altar and go. First be reconciled to your brother, and then come and offer your gift. Come to terms quickly with your accuser..." (Mathew 5:23-25 esv). If someone has hurt you, then go to God. You don't need to go to the offender to forgive them, and in many cases that would be unadvisable. Your need to forgive another is primarily an issue between you and God. However, if you have offended another, you must go to them and ask for their forgiveness and make amends when appropriate. The following are steps to seeking forgiveness:

1. Be certain about what you did that was wrong and why it was wrong.

2. Make sure you have forgiven them for whatever they have done to you.

3. Think through exactly how you will ask them to forgive you.

4. Be sure to state that what you did was wrong.

5. Be specific and admit that you did it.

6. Don't offer any excuses or try to defend yourself.

7. Place no blame on any others.

8. Don't expect that they will ask *you* to forgive them or let that be what motivates you to go to them.

9. Your confession should lead to the direct question, "Will you forgive me?"

10. Seek the right place and the right time, but the sooner the better.

11. Ask for forgiveness in person, face-to-face whenever possible and safe.

12. Unless there is no other option, do not write a letter. It can be misunderstood, and others may see it who are not involved, and it could be used against you in a court case or otherwise.

"If possible, so far as it depends on you, live peacefully with all" (Romans 12:18), but it doesn't always depend on you. If the other person doesn't want to be reconciled, it won't happen. Reconciliation between two people requires repentance and forgiveness by both parties. Rarely is there one who is completely innocent. However, if you have forgiven the other person and genuinely asked their forgiveness, then you have done all God requires of you. Be at peace with God.

Prayer for Restoration of Broken Relationships

Dear Heavenly Father, I confess and repent of my sins against my neighbor (spouse, parents, children, relatives, friends, neighbors, brothers and sisters in Christ). Thank You for Your forgiveness. I forgive them for what they have done to me, and I choose not to hold it against them in the future. I ask that You bless them and enable them to live with the consequences of my sin against them. I pray that You would heal the wounds from the sins I have inflicted on them. I ask the same for myself that I may be set free from the consequences of their sin or that You would give me the grace to live with the consequences without bitterness. I pray that You would heal my wounds and set me free so that I can live in peaceful co-existence with my neighbors and with You. In Jesus's name I pray. Amen.

CHAPTER EIGHT

SINS OF THE FATHERS

●

> [Paul] does not say, "Love your children." Nature itself takes care of this by implanting this in us even against our will. So that interpretation would be superfluous. Instead, what does he say? "Do not make your children angry." So many parents do this. They do this by depriving them of their portion of the inheritance and their promises, by oppressing them with burdens, by treating them not as though they were free but as slaves.
>
> Chrysostom, *Commentary on Ephesians* 6:4 (c. 395)

When people ask us for help we want to hear their story, and we begin by saying, "Tell me about your mom and dad and their parents. Were they believers or unbelievers?" We want to have a rough idea of what their family history is. Is there any cult or occult involvement? Does the family have any repeated patterns of sin? When they agree to be led through the Steps, inquirers pray and ask God to reveal to their minds who they need to forgive. The first two people mentioned 95 percent of the time are mom and dad. They probably aren't the two most evil people in their lives, but they are the most significant, especially in the early years of their maturation. In the quote above, Chrysostom said parents, but Paul puts the onus on fathers to bring up the children in discipline and instruction of the Lord and to do so without provoking them to anger (Ephesians 6:4). Conflicts are inevitable in every home, and learning how to handle them will either provoke anger or bring peaceful resolution. How we face conflicts reflects how much we value relationships and how important it is for us to accomplish our goals. On that basis you can identify conflict management styles as shown below:

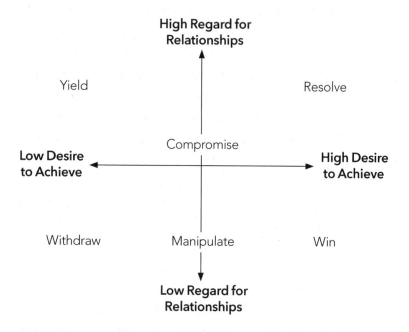

Those who have a high desire to achieve but a low regard for relationships will approach conflict with the goal of winning. If they don't care about either, they will likely withdraw from the conflict. Those who have low regard for relationships and shy away from direct confrontation will try to manipulate others to accomplish their goals.

Those who have a high regard for relationships will seek to resolve conflicts if they desire to accomplish something meaningful. Those who seek middle ground will work toward a compromise. Finally, some will yield to others when conflicts arise in order to keep the peace. There is no single right way to approach every conflict. We could write a book on this subject alone, but for the sake of this discussion we will focus on two issues.

First, which of the above conflict styles are more likely to be identified with secure people? In other words, what is more important, having a high regard for relationships or achieving our goals? Clearly those who walk away from others, try to manipulate others, or seek to win at all costs are more insecure than those who seek to resolve conflicts, work toward compromise, or yield to others. A sense of security is more apt to come from meaningful relationships than accomplishments. The most secure people are those who love God and love others. "Blessed are the peacemakers, for they shall be called sons of God" (Matthew 5:9).

How many verses can you find in the Bible that say you have to be right, first, tops, or win in every circumstance? How many verses can you find in the Bible that say we should be loving, kind, merciful, patient, forgiving, accepting, and gentle? When the price for winning costs us meaningful relationships, the price is too high. Yielding or compromising to keep the peace when something can and should be resolved will also be costly in the long run. We can sweep issues under the carpet for a time, but eventually we will trip over them. We should strive to resolve conflicts the moment they arise whenever possible. Conflicts handled incorrectly can lead to stalemates rather than decisions and ultimately damage our relationships. Whether the conflict is constructive or destructive is determined by the following:

Conflict is destructive when...	Conflict is constructive when...
we do not understand the value of conflict that naturally comes when other opinions and perspectives are shared.	we understand the need to hear the other side so responsible decisions can be made.

Conflict is destructive when...	Conflict is constructive when...
there is a competitive climate that implies a win-lose situation.	there is a cooperative spirit and commitment to seek a win-win situation.
getting my own way is all-important.	doing it God's way is all-important.
we employ all kinds of defense mechanisms, including projection, suppression, blame, withdrawal, and aggression.	we aren't defensive and assume that disagreements evolve from the other person's sincere concern for the matter.
we are locked into our own perspective and unwilling to consider the other's.	we believe that a final agreement is better than any one individual's suggestion.
we resort to personal attacks instead of focusing on issues.	disagreements are confined to issues rather than personalities.
personal ideas and opinions are valued over relationships.	relationships are more important than the need to win.

Second, which conflict style typified your father? Your mother? You? Chances are you deal with conflict the same way one of your parents did, or you are trying not to be like one or both of them. Maybe you despised the angry tempers and cruel words of your parents and vowed to never be like them. There is a problem with saying, "I am not going to be like my dad or my mother." It is still your mom or dad determining how you respond. Such vows should be renounced. We should become like Christ, and not try to be or not be like someone else.

Unless we make concerted efforts to do otherwise, we will perpetuate the habits, customs, and traditions passed on in our families for generations. We will discipline our children the way we were disciplined, unless we learn otherwise. The families we were born into and the way we have been raised have shaped our present beliefs and behaviors. Some of those family traits can be very good and others not so good. Our natural personalities and temperaments have been mostly established by the time we are five years old, and nobody has contributed more to our early development than our parents. Thankfully our Heavenly Father has the power to remake us.

It is common to hear statements like, "He is a chip off the old block," or "He's the spittin' image of his old man." The latter is slang meaning that someone is in the spirit and in the image of an ancestor. Others have said, "If you want to know what your wife will look like in twenty years, take a look at her mother," or "His family is nothing but a bunch of horse thieves."

Every family has their unique history of strengths and weaknesses that are passed on from one generation to another. Jesus said, "A pupil is not above his teacher; but everyone, after he has been fully trained, will be like his teacher" (Luke 6:40). This generational connection is clearly observed in cycles of abuse, which is a well attested social phenomenon. The abused become abusers. Whether this cycle is passed on genetically, environmentally, or spiritually is the question. Secular theorists only consider the first two possibilities. Is it nature, nurture, or the supernatural that shapes the next generation? We believe it is all three.

First, we can be genetically predisposed to certain strengths and weaknesses. For instance, it is known that some people are more prone to becoming alcoholics than others. The average person may drink socially for many years and never develop an addiction, while others can be hooked in just a few years. They weren't born alcoholics, nor are they doomed to be one. They became addicted to alcohol by choosing to drink as a means of coping, reducing stress, dealing with pain, or to get rid of inhibitions so they can party. Others with the same genetic predisposition didn't become alcoholics because they made better choices. There is very little that we can do about our genes other than to recognize our strengths and limitations, accept ourselves for who we really are physically, and be wise in the decisions that we make.

Second, the environment we were raised in is the biggest contributor to our development. This process of learning is far more caught than taught. The actions of our parents have spoken louder than their words. If you were raised in a home where pornography was left around the house, you will struggle with lust more than the person who was raised in a morally responsible home. If we are raised by angry parents who argue a lot, we just might think that is normal behavior.

The third element of development is the spiritual influence of our ancestors for good and evil. In the Ten Commandments, God said, "You shall not make for yourself an idol, or any likeness of what is in heaven above or on the earth beneath or in the water under the earth. You shall not worship them or serve them; for I, the LORD your God, am a jealous God, visiting the iniquity of the fathers on the children, on the third and the fourth generations of those who hate Me, but showing lovingkindness to thousands, to those who love Me and keep My commandments" (Exodus 20:4-6, see also Deuteronomy 5:9-10; Exodus 34:6-7; Deuteronomy 7:9-10; Numbers 14:18). These citations affirm that God blesses those who are obedient to His covenant to the thousandth generation but the iniquities of those who are disobedient are passed on to the third and fourth generations.

We are not guilty because of our parents' sins, but because they sinned, we are vulnerable to what they have taught and modeled for us. Jeremiah wrote: "Ah Lord GOD! Behold, You have made the heavens and the earth by Your great power and by Your outstretched arm! Nothing is too difficult for You, who shows lovingkindness to thousands, but repays the iniquity of fathers *into the bosom* of their children after them, O great and mighty God. The LORD of hosts is His name" (Jeremiah 32:17-18 emphasis added). Whatever is being passed on from one generation to the next is not due to the external environment, because it occurs in the bosom of the next generation, and there is no genetic explanation for the passing on of iniquities.

Consider the words in Leviticus 26:38-42 concerning the sins of our fathers: "And you shall perish among the nations, and the land of your enemies shall eat you up. And those of you who are left shall rot away in your enemies' lands because of their iniquity, and also because of the iniquities of their fathers they shall rot away like them. But if they confess their iniquity and the iniquity of their fathers in their treachery that they committed against me, and also in walking contrary to me…if then their uncircumcised heart is humbled and they make amends for their iniquity, then I will remember my covenant…" (ESV). Confessing the iniquities of our fathers will not have any effect on us genetically, but it will spiritually.

In the Old Testament God's people were instructed to confess their sins and iniquities and those of their ancestors. Iniquities relate more to a rebellious spirit or strong will. Somehow these iniquities are passed on from one generation to another. One Old Testament scholar wrote the following:

> An important consideration is the distinction between corporate and individual responsibility for sin. In its early development Israel was very much influenced by a dynamic concept of corporate sin…The family group was a much more significant entity than the individual person. When the head of such a group transgressed, he transmitted guilt to every member of it…Thus,

according to the Decalogue (see Exodus 20:5; Deut. 5:9; cf. Exodus 34:7; Num. 14:18), the iniquity of the father is to be visited upon the children.[1]

In the context of idolatry, Hosea mentions demonic spirits affecting children, which are related to parents' sins:

> My people inquire of a piece of wood, and their walking staff gives them oracles. For a spirit of whoredom has led them astray, and they have left their God to play the whore. They sacrifice on the tops of the mountains and burn offerings on the hills, under oak, poplar, and terebinth, because their shade is good. Therefore your daughters play the whore, and your brides commit adultery (Hosea 4:12-13 ESV).

The cause of the children's sin of adultery and prostitution is not only the parents' sin of idolatry, but also the demonic "spirit of prostitution." Notice the examples of how to deal with ancestral sins in the Old Testament: Those of Israelite descent had separated themselves from all foreigners. They stood in their places and confessed their sins and the wickedness of their fathers (Nehemiah 9:2).

Nehemiah prayed, "I confess the sins we Israelites, including myself and my father's family, have committed against you" (1:6 NIV).

Jeremiah prayed, "We acknowledge our wickedness, LORD, and the guilt of our ancestors; we have indeed sinned against you" (Jeremiah 14:20 NIV).

Daniel prayed, "We have not obeyed the LORD our God or kept the laws he gave us through his servants the prophets. All Israel has transgressed your law and turned away, refusing to obey you. Therefore the curses and sworn judgments written in the Law of Moses, the servant of God, have been poured out on us, because we have sinned against you" (Daniel 9:10-11 NIV).

God had spoken and the prophets had warned the people about generational sins. In the early sixth century BC, the prophet Ezekiel had to correct an abuse of this generational curse:

> The word of the LORD came to me: "What do you people mean by quoting this proverb about the land of Israel: 'The parents eat sour grapes, and the children's teeth are set on edge?' As surely as I live, declares the Sovereign LORD, you will no longer quote this proverb in Israel" (Ezekiel 18:1-3 NIV).

The popular proverb was not from the book of Proverbs nor from the mouth of God. The problem Ezekiel was trying to correct was a fatalistic response to the law and the abdication of personal responsibility. Children are not guilty because of their parents' sins and they will not be punished for their parents' iniquities, which are visited upon them, if they are diligent to turn away from the sins of their parents. Scholars have shown this to be the case:

> The corporate involvement of sin deeply impressed itself upon the people, however. The prophets proclaimed that it was not only a few wicked individuals, but the whole nation, that was laden with sin (see Isaiah 1:4). Generation upon generation treasured up wrath. Thus it was easy for those who were finally forced to bear the painful consequences to protest that all the effects of corporate guilt were being visited upon them. The exiles lamented: "Our fathers sinned, and are no more; it is we who have borne their iniquities" (Lamentations 5:7). They even had a proverb: "The fathers have eaten sour grapes, and the children's teeth are set on edge." Against this both Jeremiah and Ezekiel protested (see Jeremiah 31:29,30; Ezekiel 18:10-20). No son was to be held accountable for his father's crimes. "The soul who sins shall die" (Ezekiel 18:4). In saying this, they did not mean to deny

corporate sin: this was beyond dispute. Their purpose was to accentuate individual responsibility, which was in danger of becoming submerged in a consciousness of overpowering national calamity. Even though the nation was now suffering a bitter corporate punishment, there was hope for the individual if he would repent.[2]

Under the old covenant, all of God's chosen people were called to repent of their sins and iniquities regardless of whether the scope of their offenses was personal or national. National or corporate repentance cannot happen without individual repentance. We have seen in the Old Testament the transmission of sin from one generation to the next and how the prophets called the people to confess their sins and the sins of their fathers. The apostle Peter would likely urge you to do the same, "knowing that you were ransomed from the futile ways inherited from your forefathers" (1 Peter 1:18 ESV). The apostle Paul would add, "Just as sin entered the world through one man, and death through sin, and in this way death came to all men, because all have sinned" (Romans 5:12 NIV).

A television documentary illustrated how iniquities can be passed on to the next generation if not dealt with. A high school girl in a small hamlet in southern Germany decided to do a report on the role her town played in World War II. She had always been told that her town had resisted Hitler and that the Catholic Church had instructed its people not to pray for him.

What she discovered in the local library was just the opposite. The town had acquiesced to Hitler's regime. Her report brought quick disclaimers from town leaders and warnings not to dig up any more dirt. She felt betrayed by her ancestors. After high school she married and did much more extensive research. She printed her report in the local paper. The whole town turned against her when she reported her findings. Her husband left her, her family deserted her, and she was eventually run out of town. She is now living somewhere in North America.

If you have been following the news, then you know that anti-Semitism is on the rise again in Germany, Europe, and around the world. How can that be? Haven't we learned anything from the past? How could something so sinful be on the rise again? There could be other reasons, but we believe part of the cause is due to a lack of complete repentance. People covered it up. Some even deny the Holocaust took place! Those who will not acknowledge the sins of their fathers may be doomed to repeat them.

After the nation of Israel split, every king in the northern kingdom of Israel continued in the sins of Jeroboam. None of them had to. Any one of them could have said, "Jeroboam was wrong, we should go back to Jerusalem and worship God the way He instructed David." But none did, and Israel perished as a kingdom.

A mother with a child in her arms and a husband by her side approached me at a conference. She had read many of our books and worked through the *Steps to Freedom in Christ* on her own. She believed that one more issue needed to be resolved.

"My parents and their parents bad-mouthed every pastor in every church we ever went to, and I have done the same," she told me. "I don't want my child to repeat this same sin, so I am confessing my sin and the sin of my ancestors to you as a member of the clergy. Would you forgive me?" What a courageous and marvelous thing she did for herself and for her child!

Jesus said to those who were carrying on the sinful traditions of their forefathers:

> Behold, I am sending you prophets and wise men and scribes; some of them you will kill and crucify, and some of them you will scourge in your synagogues, and persecute from city to city, so that upon you may fall the guilt

of all the righteous blood shed on earth, from the blood of righteous Abel to the blood of Zechariah, the son of Berechiah, whom you murdered between the temple and the altar. Truly I say to you, all these things will come upon this generation (Matthew 23:34-36).

Jesus tells the Pharisees and teachers of the law that upon them will come all the righteous blood from Abel to Zechariah. This was a prophecy that was fulfilled in the destruction of the Temple and the scattering of the Jewish people. The phrase, "Fill up, then, the measure of the guilt of your fathers" (Matthew 23:32), infers that God's toleration is self-limited, after which both ancestral and present sin overflow together in divine judgment. Jesus's words about multigenerational guilt cannot be ignored.

New Creations but Personally Responsible

Blood runs thick in family lines. We naturally stick together as families and defend ourselves against those who threaten us. We advise newlyweds to refrain from being critical about their spouse's family. You can and should critique your own, but don't put your spouse in a positon of having to choose between you and his or her family. You didn't marry Adam and Eve before the fall, you married one of their fallen descendants. Both husband and wife come to a marriage with three or four generations of family habits, traditions, and customs. Each is responsible for what they bring. The value for confessing the sins of your ancestors is to acknowledge that they weren't perfect and to stop defending the indefensible. Some are actually unaware that what was modeled at home was sinful, such as the way they talked to each other, and the way they talked about others. One man saw his father physically abuse his mother and was told that is how to keep a wife in line. He did likewise until his wife turned him in.

A pastor's wife was referred to me. She was on staff at their church and appeared very professional, but she had some real anger issues. After hearing her story I couldn't see anything in her past that would be the basis for her present struggles. There were no major traumas or moral failures. According to her, she was raised in a fine Christian home and never deviated from a Christian lifestyle. I asked if she would like to be led through the Steps, and she agreed. The change was astounding, and everybody at the church wondered what happened to her. On the way out of my office she stopped at the door, turned around, and said, "It wasn't a good Christian home, was it?" It all surfaced as she forgave her mom and dad.

Our first Canadian directors had just finished a conference in Saskatchewan and joined me in Toronto. They were visibly shaken by what they had experienced the previous week. Every individual freedom appointment dealt with spiritual abuse. Wives and children were beaten by elders in their church in the name of discipline, and it had been going on for generations.

Much of Asia is steeped in ancestor worship, which creates a real problem for each new generation. A Korean student was struggling with a family "tradition." When he went home to visit his parents he was expected to come before his father who would be sitting in a chair, and go to his knees before him until his father released him. Is that just a cultural way of showing respect to our elders? I asked his permission to discuss that question in class where there were other Korean students. They were reluctant to admit it at first, but they too were expected to do the same. The whole class believed that such behavior is rooted more in ancestor worship than just a spiritually neutral, customary way of showing respect. Many Asians willing to go through the Steps struggle to forgive their parents because that would be admitting that they did something wrong.

There are numerous kinds of iniquities that can be environmentally and spiritually passed on from one generation to another. Such sins and iniquities can be the roots of sexual addiction and perversion, alcoholism and drugs, violent behavior, and more. There are also family traits such as pride in achievement, materialism, intellectualism, social prestige, independence, control, perfectionism, mental illness, anger, rage, or unforgiveness. It isn't our purpose to place blame or to categorize the root cause of every problem. Many of these strongholds have already been dealt with in previous Steps.

What people need to know is that they can be free in Christ from inherited or acquired bondages linked to generational sin if they will repent. When we lead people through the Steps, God often brings issues to people's minds that they had completely forgotten about. It really isn't a question of trying to remember. It is more a case of God revealing to our minds what we need to do in order to repent. Sometimes God reveals what has been going on in our ancestry that was previously unknown, as the following testimony illustrates:

> I thought my story was unique, but I often wondered if anyone else had the spiritual conflicts I was suffering with. My problem began a couple of years ago. I was experiencing terribly demonic nightmares and had nights in which I felt the presence of something, or someone in my room. One night I woke up feeling like someone was choking me and I could not speak or say the name of Jesus. I was terrified.
>
> I sought help from church leaders and pastors. They had no idea how to encourage me. Eventually fear turned into panic anxiety disorder and my thoughts were so loud, destructive, and frightening that I visited my primary care provider. I thought for sure she would understand my belief that this was a spiritual battle. When I expressed the idea that the enemy was attacking me, she responded by diagnosing me with a bipolar disorder and

told me that I would be on medication for the rest of my life. She also gave me a prescription for anti-depressants and anti-anxiety meds. I was devastated.

I told my husband the diagnosis and he assured me that it wasn't true. I decided not to take the medication. I just didn't have any peace about it. My pastors prayed over me, but nothing changed. I began Christian counseling, which helped a bit, but it was nowhere near worth the $400 per month that I paid. When I told my Christian counselor about what was happening in my mind, and about my fears, she too said, "I think it is time for medication." It seemed like everyone thought I was crazy. No one believed that my problem was spiritual.

Thankfully, I came across one of your books and read stories of people I could relate to. I knew there was an answer. It was in that book that I first heard of "the *Steps to Freedom in Christ.*" Honestly, I was afraid of the Steps at first. I didn't know what to expect, but one of our pastors had recently met Dr. Anderson and was learning how to lead people through the Steps. He offered to help me and I accepted.

Going through the Steps was one of the most difficult, yet incredible things I've ever done. I experienced a lot of interference, such as a headache and confusion, but having the Holy Spirit reveal to me all that I needed to renounce was incredible. When I prayed and asked God to bring to my mind the sins of my ancestors I was shocked at all that came up. I don't even know my ancestors! I later asked my mother about the things that came to my mind during the session and she confirmed that my family had been involved in those things. I was amazed by how the Holy Spirit brought out the truth.

After going through the Steps my mind was completely silent. It was amazing. There were no nagging thoughts. I was totally at peace. I wanted to cry with joy. After that I wasn't afraid of being alone, and the nightmares were gone. I didn't have to play the radio or television to drown out the terrible thoughts. I could sit in silence and be still.[3]

Curses

Curses are a blasphemous pronouncement, oath, or swearing intended to bring injury to a person. Another person could swear at you, but it would have little effect on you unless you believed it. Saying to a child that he or she will never amount to anything can seem like nothing more than words said in anger, but it can have a devastating effect if the child believes that he or she will never amount to anything.

Spiritual curses are common in developing countries that practice spiritism, voodoo, magic, and pagan rituals. Curses are also present in North America when people get involved in the dark side of the supernatural. Summoning and sending demons is a central part of satanic rituals. If you have ever been abruptly awakened at a certain time of the night, like 3:00 a.m., you have probably been targeted. In every conference I have conducted in the United States, at least a third of those attending say that has happened to them. It is no sin to be targeted, and it will have no lasting negative effect on you if you just ignore it and go back to sleep. If the attack persists, then submit to God, resist the devil, and he will flee from you (James 4:7).

Predictions given by a medium, or even things unwisely said or done by a parent, can be used by Satan. His accusations will function like a curse on your life if you believe them. When playing with a Ouija board or Magic Eight Ball, a message or response is often believed. The person may, either consciously or unconsciously, feel helplessly bound to their assessments or predictions. (Hopefully, this was dealt with in the first Step.)

We encourage you to take your place in Christ, put on the armor of God, and stand firm against all assignments and weapons formed against you. Christ is our defense, and we should never let the devil set the agenda. Please take this last Step very seriously. It is our desire that you come under the protection and authority of Christ, and by the grace of God break any link to the bondages of generational sins and curses. Are you just a victim of your past? "No, in all these things we are more than conquerors through him who loved us" (Romans 8:37 ESV).

Discussion Questions

1. What did you learn from each of your parents on how to deal with conflicts?

2. Which did each of your parents value most: high regard for relationships or high need to achieve?

3. How has the example of your parents affected you?

4. What is the potential harm in defending your family?

5. What is the value of confessing our sins and the sins of our ancestors?

6. Why is it wrong to blame our parents for our sins?

7. Why is it wise not to attack your spouse's family?

8. What examples can you think of in which families, churches, denominations, corporations, and countries have covered up past sins? What is the lasting effect of that?

9. Other than idolatry, what is wrong with ancestor worship, and how can it effect those who practice it?

10. If you believe that you have been cursed, what can you do about it?

Steps to Freedom in Christ

Curses Versus Blessings

The Bible declares that the iniquities of one generation can be visited on to the third and fourth generations of those who hate God, but God's blessings will be poured out on thousands of generations of those who love and obey Him (Exodus 20:4-6). The iniquities of one generation can adversely affect future ones, unless those sins are renounced and your new spiritual heritage in Christ is claimed. This cycle of abuse and all negative influences can be stopped through genuine repentance. You are not guilty of your ancestor's sins, but because of their sins you have been affected by their influence. Jesus said that after we have been fully trained, we will be like our teachers (Luke 6:40), and Peter wrote that you were redeemed "from your futile way of life inherited from your forefathers" (1 Peter 1:18). Ask the Lord to reveal your ancestral sins and then renounce them as follows:

> *Dear Heavenly Father, please reveal to my mind all the sins of my ancestors that have been passed down through family lines. Since I am a new creation in Christ, I want to experience my freedom from those influences and walk in my new identity as a child of God. In Jesus's name I pray. Amen.*

Listen carefully to what the Holy Spirit may reveal, and list anything that comes to your mind. God may reveal cult and occultic religious practices of your ancestors that you were not aware of. Also, every family has history of mental illnesses, sicknesses, divorce, sexual sins, anger, depression, fear, violence, abuse, etc. When nothing else comes to mind, conclude with:

> **Lord, I renounce**… (name all the family sins that God brings to your mind).

We cannot passively take our place in Christ; we must actively and intentionally choose to submit to God, resist the devil, and then he will flee from us. Verbally complete this final Step with the following declaration and prayer:

Declaration

> *I here and now reject and disown all the sins of my ancestors. As one who has been delivered from the domain of darkness and transferred into the kingdom of God's Son, I declare myself to be free from those harmful influences. I am no longer "in Adam." I am now alive "in Christ." Therefore I am the recipient of the blessings of God upon my life as I choose to love and obey Him. As one who has been crucified and raised with Christ and who sits with Him in heavenly places, I renounce any and all satanic attacks and assignments directed against me and my ministry. Every curse placed on me was broken when Christ became a curse for me by dying on the cross (Galatians 3:13). I reject any and every way in which Satan may claim ownership of me. I belong to the Lord Jesus Christ who purchased me with His own precious blood. I declare myself to be fully and eternally signed over and committed to the Lord Jesus Christ. Therefore, having submitted to God, I now by His authority resist the devil, and I command every spiritual enemy of the Lord Jesus Christ to leave my presence. I put on the armor of God and I stand against Satan's temptations, accusations, and deceptions. From this day forward I will seek to do only the will of my Heavenly Father.*

Prayer

> *Dear Heavenly Father, I come to You as Your child, bought out of slavery to sin by the blood of the Lord Jesus Christ. You are the Lord of the universe and the Lord of my life. I submit*

my body to You as a living and holy sacrifice. May You be glorified through my life and body. I now ask You to fill me with Your Holy Spirit. I commit myself to the renewing of my mind in order that I may prove that Your will is good, acceptable, and perfect for me. I desire nothing more than to be like You. I pray, believe, and do all this in the wonderful name of Jesus, my Lord and Savior. Amen.

Incomplete Resolution?

After you have completed the Steps, close your eyes and sit silently for a minute or two. Is it quiet in your mind? Most will sense the peace of God and a clear mind. A small percentage of believers don't, and usually they know that there is still some unfinished business with God. If you believe that you have been totally honest with God and processed all the Steps to the best of your ability, then ask God as follows:

Dear Heavenly Father, I earnestly desire Your presence, and I am asking You to reveal to my mind what is keeping me from experiencing that. I ask that You take me back to times of trauma in my life and show me the lies that I have believed. I pray that You will grant me the repentance that leads to a knowledge of the truth that will set me free. I humbly ask that You would heal my damaged emotions. In Jesus's name I pray. Amen

Don't spend your time trying to figure out what is wrong with you if nothing new surfaces. You are only responsible to deal with what you know. Instead, commit yourself to finding out what is right about you, and who you are in Christ. Some believers can sense a newfound freedom and then days or weeks later begin to struggle again. Chances are God is revealing some more of your past that needs to be dealt with. God reveals one layer at a time for those who have experienced severe trauma. Trying to deal with every abuse in one setting may be too overwhelming for some. If we show ourselves faithful in little things, God will put us in charge of bigger things. Claim your place in Christ with the following:

"I renounce the lie that I am rejected, unloved, or shameful. In Christ I am accepted." God says:

> I am God's child (John 1:12)
>
> I am Christ's friend (John 15:15)
>
> I have been justified (Romans 5:1)
>
> I am united with the Lord and I am one spirit with Him (1 Corinthians 6:17)
>
> I have been bought with a price; I belong to God (1 Corinthians 6:19-20)
>
> I am a member of Christ's body (1 Corinthians 12:27)
>
> I am a saint, a holy one (Ephesians 1:1)
>
> I have been adopted as God's child (Ephesians 1:5)
>
> I have direct access to God through the Holy Spirit (Ephesians 2:18)
>
> I have been redeemed and forgiven of all my sins (Colossians 1:14)
>
> I am complete in Christ (Colossians 2:10)

"I renounce the lie that I am guilty, unprotected, alone, or abandoned. In Christ I am secure." God says:

> I am free from condemnation (Romans 8:1-2)

I am assured that all things work together for good (Romans 8:28)

I am free from any condemning charges against me (Romans 8:31-34)

I cannot be separated from the love of God (Romans 8:35-39)

I have been established, anointed, and sealed by God (2 Corinthians 1:21-22)

I am confident that the good work God has begun in me will be perfected (Philippians 1:6)

I am a citizen of heaven (Philippians 3:20)

I am hidden with Christ in God (Colossians 3:3)

I have not been given a spirit of fear, but of power, love, and self-control (2 Timothy 1:7)

I can find grace and mercy to help in time of need (Hebrews 4:16)

I am born of God and the evil one cannot touch me (1 John 5:18)

"I renounce the lie that I am worthless, inadequate, helpless, or hopeless. In Christ I am significant." God says:

I am the salt of the earth and the light of the world (Matthew 5:13-14)

I am a branch of the true vine, Jesus, a channel of His life (John 15:1,5)

I have been chosen and appointed by God to bear fruit (John 15:16)

I am a personal, Spirit-empowered witness of Christ's (Acts 1:8)

I am a temple of God (1 Corinthians 3:16)

I am a minister of reconciliation for God (2 Corinthians 5:17-21)

I am a fellow worker with God (2 Corinthians 6:1)

I am seated with Christ in the heavenly realms (Ephesians 2:6)

I am God's workmanship, created for good works (Ephesians 2:10)

I may approach God with freedom and confidence (Ephesians 3:12)

I can do all things through Christ who strengthens me! (Philippians 4:13)

I am not the great "I Am," but by the grace of God I am what I am (See Exodus 3:14; John 8:24,28,58; 1 Corinthians 15:10)

Maintaining Your Freedom

It is exciting to experience your freedom in Christ, but what you have gained must be maintained. You have won an important battle, but the war goes on. To maintain your freedom in Christ and grow as a disciple of Jesus in the grace of God, you must continue renewing your mind to the truth of God's Word. If you become aware of lies that you have believed, renounce them and choose the truth. If more painful memories surface, then forgive those who hurt you and renounce any sinful part you played. Many people choose to go through the *Steps to Freedom in Christ* again on their own to make sure they have dealt with all their issues. Often new issues will surface. The process can assist you in a regular "house cleaning." It is not uncommon after going through the Steps for people to have thoughts like: *Nothing has really changed. You're the same person you always were. It didn't work.* In most cases you should just ignore it. We are not called to dispel the darkness, we are called to turn on the light. You don't get rid of negative thoughts by rebuking every one, you get rid of them by repenting and choosing the truth.

In the introduction to this book, you were encouraged to write down any false beliefs and lies that surfaced during the Steps. For the next 40 days, verbally work through that list saying, I renounce (the lies you have believed), and I announce the truth that (what you have chosen to believe is true based on God's Word).

We encourage you to read *Victory Over the Darkness* and *The Bondage Breaker* if you haven't already done so or to go through The Freedom in Christ Course. The 21-day devotional *Walking in Freedom* was written for those who have gone through the Steps. To continue growing in the grace of God we suggest the following:

1. Get rid of or destroy any cult or occult objects in your home. (See Acts 19:18-20.)

2. Be part of a church where God's truth is taught with kindness and grace, and get involved in a small group where you can be honest and real.

3. Read and meditate on the truth of God's Word each day.

4. Don't let your mind be passive, especially concerning what you watch and listen to (internet, music, TV, etc.). Actively take every thought captive to the obedience of Christ.

5. Be a good steward of your health and develop a godly lifestyle of rest, exercise, and proper diet.

6. Say the following daily prayer for the next 40 days and the other prayers as needed.

Daily Prayer and Declaration

Dear Heavenly Father, I praise You and honor You as my Lord and Savior. You are in control of all things. I thank You that You are always with me and will never leave me nor forsake me. You are the only all-powerful and only wise God. You are kind and loving in all Your ways. I love You and thank You that I am united with Jesus and spiritually alive in Him. I choose not to love the world or the things in the world, and I crucify the flesh and all its passions. Thank You for the life I now have in Christ. I ask You to fill me with the Holy Spirit so I can be guided by You and not carry out the desires of the flesh. I declare my total dependence upon You, and I take my stand against Satan and all his lying ways. I choose to believe the truth of God's Word despite what my feelings may say. I refuse to be discouraged; You are the God of all hope. Nothing is too difficult for You. I am confident that You will supply all my needs as I seek to live according to Your Word. I thank You that I can be content and live a responsible life through Christ who strengthens me.

I now take my stand against Satan and command him and all his evil spirits to depart from me. I choose to put on the full armor of God so I may be able to stand firm against all the devil's schemes. I submit my body as a living and holy sacrifice to You, and I choose to renew my mind by Your living Word. By so doing I will be able to prove that Your will is good, acceptable, and perfect for me. In the name of my Lord and Savior, Jesus Christ, I pray. Amen.

Bedtime Prayer

Thank You, Lord, that You have brought me into Your family and have blessed me with every spiritual blessing in the heavenly places in Christ Jesus. Thank You for this time of renewal and refreshment through sleep. I accept it as one of Your blessings for Your children, and I trust You to guard my mind and my body during my sleep. As I have thought about You and Your truth during the day, I choose to let those good thoughts continue in my mind while I am asleep. I commit myself to You for Your protection against every attempt of Satan and his demons to attack me during sleep. Guard my mind from nightmares. I renounce all fear and cast every anxiety upon You. I commit myself to You as my rock, my fortress, and my strong tower. May Your peace be upon this place of rest. In the strong name of the Lord Jesus Christ I pray. Amen.

Prayer for Spiritual Cleansing of Home/Apartment/Room

After removing and destroying all objects of false worship, pray this prayer aloud in every room:

Dear Heavenly Father, I acknowledge that You are the Lord of heaven and earth. In Your sovereign power and love, You have entrusted many things to me. Thank You for this place to live. I claim my home as a place of spiritual safety for me and my family and ask for Your protection from all the attacks of the enemy. As a child of God, raised up and seated with Christ in the heavenly places, I command every evil spirit claiming ground in this place, based on the activities of past or present occupants, including me and my family, to leave and never return. I renounce all demonic assignments directed against this place. I ask You, Heavenly Father, to post Your holy angels around this place to guard it from any and all attempts of the enemy to enter and disturb Your purposes for me and my family. I thank You for doing this in the name of the Lord Jesus Christ. Amen.

Prayer for Living in a Non-Christian Environment

After removing and destroying all objects of false worship from your possession, pray this aloud in the place where you live:

Thank You, Heavenly Father, for a place to live and to be renewed by sleep. I ask You to set aside my room (or portion of this room) as a place of spiritual safety for me. I renounce any allegiance given to false gods or spirits by other occupants. I renounce any claim to this room (space) by Satan based on the activities of past or present occupants, including me. On the basis of my position as a child of God and joint heir with Christ, who has all authority in heaven and on earth, I command all evil spirits to leave this place and never return. I ask You, Heavenly Father, to station Your holy angels to protect me while I live here. In Jesus's mighty name I pray. Amen.

CHAPTER NINE

LIVING BY THE SPIRIT

●

> The whole essence of the Gospel is to think according to the Spirit, to live according to the Spirit, to believe according to the Spirit, to have nothing of the flesh in one's mind and acts and life. That means also to have no hope in the flesh. "Walk then," he says, "in the Spirit"—that is, "Be alive. If you do so you will not consummate the desires of the flesh. You will admit into consciousness no sin, which is born of the flesh."
>
> Marcus Victorinus (c. 280)

God is love and Jesus is the truth. Without the love of God, we would never know the truth. Without the truth, we would never know the love of God. We cannot diminish one attribute of God without distorting the others. When we disjoin love from the character of God, we diminish truth. God is righteous, but He is also merciful. Emphasizing God's mercy over justice leads to license. Emphasizing God's justice over mercy leads to legalism, which has plagued the church since its beginning. It is hard to say who is angrier. Is it the controlling legalist who is mad at liberals for pushing their promiscuous social agenda, or the progressive liberal who is hostile toward anyone who disapproves of their immoral behavior?

We asked the George Barna Research Group to conduct a nationwide survey of adult believers. We wanted to know how widespread legalism is in the American church. This survey, "Christian Beliefs About Spiritual Life and the Church," asked people to respond to six different statements with "strongly agree," "somewhat agree," "somewhat disagree," strongly disagree," or "don't know." One of the survey statements was, "The Christian life is well summed-up as 'trying hard to do what God commands.'" If you strongly agree with that statement you would be in the majority, for 57 percent of the respondents strongly agreed and 25 percent somewhat agreed. Maybe that is why the majority of respondents felt like they didn't measure up to God's expectations of them. In *Grace That Breaks the Chains*[1] [of legalism] we explain how legalism is still plaguing the church and provide some steps to help struggling believers break the chains of legalism. Transitioning from law to grace is moving from "got to" to "want to," from "being driven" to "being led," from "doing" to "being," from "spiritual death" to "spiritual life."

The Old Covenant was based on the Mosaic Law. It was a conditional covenant. "If you obey the law, then…" To live a righteous life, a believer had to obey the law. The problem was that nobody could. If you are steeped in legalism, anger is inevitable because living under the law is one continuous blocked goal. You may look righteous on the outside, but inside you are plagued by guilt or denial. The New Covenant of grace is not a law to be obeyed; it is a life to be lived in freedom. The problem is that the pendulum can swing too far in the other direction and usher in a new level of promiscuity. Proclaiming the law has never worked and it never will! Tolerating sin doesn't work either. Neither legalism nor license can stem the tide of moral decay. Paul captures the balance in Galatians 5:16-18:

> I say, walk by the Spirit, and you will not carry out the desire of the flesh. For the flesh sets its desire against the

Spirit, and the Spirit against the flesh; for these are in opposition to one another, so that you may not do the things that you please. But if you are led by the Spirit, you are not under the Law.

So how do we walk or live by the Spirit? If we answered the question with three steps and a formula, we would be putting you back under the law. Moving from law to grace is moving from death to life. From lifeless deeds to the fruit of the Spirit. There is no fruit without life. The Galatians passage explains more what walking by the Spirit is not, rather than what it is. But knowing that is helpful, because it provides boundaries within which we freely live. So let's first consider what walking by the Spirit is not.

Walking by the Spirit Is Not License

"Are we to continue in sin that grace may abound?" Paul asks in Romans 6:1 (esv). Since Christ died for our sins, then sinning more would make His love and forgiveness even more extravagant. Such erroneous thinking leads to license, which is an excessive or undisciplined lifestyle constituting the abuse of a privilege. Paul answers, "By no means! How can we who died to sin still live in it" (6:2 esv)? Why would you want to go back to the bondage of sin if Christ has set you free from it?

"If you are led by the Spirit, you are not under the Law" (Galatians 5:18 esv). Does that mean we can do whatever we please? If there is no speed limit, we can drive as fast as we want. Right? That would be licentious, which means that a person lacks moral discipline and has no regard for accepted rules and regulations. If we live by the Spirit we will not do as we please, nor carry out the desires of the flesh.

When we were physically born, we were completely dependent upon our parents for survival. If they hadn't fed us, changed our diapers, and taken care of us, we would have died. Like most children, we started to exert our independence at about the age of two. Can't you just hear a little child saying, "I can do it. I want to do it myself"? So all good parents set boundaries. It is not safe or good training to let children have their own way.

When we are born again spiritually and become children of God, the presence of the Holy Spirit brings us sorrow when we try to please the flesh. If there were no moral restraints and no boundaries to govern our behavior, we would all slide into moral decadence. Paul wrote, "You were called to freedom, brethren; only do not turn your freedom into an opportunity for the flesh, but through love serve one another" (Galatians 5:13). God wants us to be free, but freedom is not license. We are free by the grace of God to become all that He created us to be and to live a responsible life.

In the first half of the twentieth century, rigid fundamentalism left many churches frozen in legalism. Beginning in the 60s, it began to thaw, and the Jesus movement was ushered in. The pendulum swung from an emphasis on the justice of God to an emphasis on the mercy and love of God, and many in the American culture went from legalism to license. Some reasoned, "Since I am under the grace of God, I can do whatever I want—and there is no way a God of love would send me to hell." So let's enjoy our freedom to have free sex and use drugs to heighten our pleasure. Being licentious always comes with a price. The number of people who have died or whose lives have been ruined through sexual disease and drug usage is staggering.

Don't confuse license with freedom. True freedom doesn't lie just in the exercise of choices, but in the consequences of the choices as well. Some might think they have the freedom to tell a lie, but they would be in bondage to that lie. They would have to remember what the lie was and to whom they told it. They may choose to rob a bank, but they would always be looking over their shoulder, fearing they may be caught. License leads to bondage.

Living by the Spirit Is Not Legalism

Living by the Spirit is not legalism either. God's grace did not do away with the Law. Jesus came to fulfill it. The moral standard of God has not changed. What changed under the New Covenant was the means by which we can live a righteous and peaceful life, a life that is free from "bitterness and wrath and anger and clamor and slander...along with all malice" (Ephesians 4:31). The Ten Commandments in the Old Testament become ten promises in the New Testament. Those who are free in Christ will not have other gods, will not kill, will not steal, will not covet, etc. If you choose to try having a relationship with God on the basis of law there are three reasons why that will fail.

Law Brings a Curse

First, according to Galatians 3:10-14 (NIV), the law will function as a curse:

> All who rely on the works of the law are under a curse, as it is written: "Cursed is everyone who does not continue to do everything written in the Book of the Law." Clearly no one who relies on the law is justified before God, because "the righteous will live by faith." The law is not based on faith; on the contrary, it says, "The person who does these things will live by them." Christ redeemed us from the curse of the law by becoming a curse for us, for it is written: "Cursed is everyone who is hung on a pole." He redeemed us in order that the blessing given to Abraham might come to the Gentiles through Christ Jesus, so that by faith we might receive the promise of the Spirit.

James wrote, "Whoever keeps the whole law and yet stumbles in one point, he has become guilty of all" (James 2:10). In addition to failing in your relationship with God, you will be a pain in the neck for yourself and others if you try by human effort to live up to the standards of the Law. We are not saved by how we perform; we are saved and sanctified by what we believe, which is the gospel and all of God's Word: "The Law has become our tutor to lead us to Christ, so that we may be justified by faith" (Galatians 3:24).

People stay away from legalistic churches because they don't want to feel guilty. We should be going to churches to get rid of the guilt. We don't motivate people by guilt, because there is no condemnation for those who are in Christ Jesus (Romans 8:1). We don't instill fear into the hearts of believers, because "God has not given us a spirit of timidity, but of power and love and discipline" (2 Timothy 1:7), and "perfect love casts out fear" (1 John 4:18). We desire that God's children live righteous lives, but they can't do this by living under law. Under the New Covenant of grace, we actually can live a righteous life by faith in the power of the Holy Spirit. "He redeemed us in order that the blessing given to Abraham might come to the Gentiles through Christ Jesus, so that by faith we might receive the promise of the Spirit" (Galatians 3:14 NIV).

Law Cannot Give Life

The second limitation of the law is that it is powerless to give life. Telling people that what they are doing is wrong does not give them the power to stop. "Is the Law then contrary to the promises of God? May it never be! For if a law had been given which was able to impart life, then righteousness would indeed have been based on law" (Galatians 3:21).

I saw an article in a paper written by a lady who was commissioned by the state to give lectures in public high schools about practicing safe sex. They believed that such teaching would stem the tide of sexually transmitted diseases and teenage pregnancies. The problem was the lady herself had a major weight problem. She had read numerous books on weight loss, nutrition, and exercise. She probably could have given a lecture on those topics as well. However, knowing that information didn't stop her from overeating. Since information alone didn't curb her appetite, how could she expect children less than half her age to do better with self-control than she did? The government sponsored a program for years to counter drug abuse. Their slogan was "Just say no!" Did that work? No!

We were dead in our trespasses and sins, but now we are alive *in Christ*—we are "servants of a new covenant, not of the letter but of the Spirit; for the letter kills, but the Spirit gives life" (2 Corinthians 3:6). This life, our union with God, establishes our true identity as children of God. Jesus said, "I came that they may have life, and have it abundantly" (John 10:10).

"To all who did receive him, who believed in his name, he gave the right to become children of God" (John 1:12 ESV). "The Spirit himself bears witness with our spirit that we are children of God" (Romans 8:16 ESV). Knowing who we are in Christ is essential for living a righteous life. "See what kind of love the Father has given to us, that we should be called children of God; and so we are. The reason why the world does not know us is that it did not know him. Beloved, we are God's children now, and what we will be has not yet appeared; but we know that when he appears we shall be like him, because we shall see him as he is. And everyone who thus hopes in him purifies himself as he is pure" (1 John 3:1-3 ESV).

We cannot consistently behave in a way that is inconsistent with what we believe about ourselves. We are not just forgiven sinners. We are new creations in Christ (2 Corinthians 5:17). We are "saints by calling, with all who in every place call on the name of the Lord

Jesus Christ, their Lord and ours" (1 Corinthians 1:2). God has changed who we are. It is our responsibility to believe that and be filled with the Holy Spirit. Why don't you ask Him right now to fill you with His Holy Spirit? Ask Him every day. Ask Him every time you stumble to fill you with the knowledge that you are already forgiven. That is how you overcome the desires of the flesh.

Law Stimulates Sinful Desires

Third, the law actually has the capacity to stimulate the desire to do what it was intended to prohibit. According to Paul, the law arouses sinful passions. "While we were in the flesh, the sinful passions, which were aroused by the Law, were at work in the members of our body to bear fruit for death" (Romans 7:5). Is the law sinful then? Not according to Paul's words in Romans 7:7-8:

> Is the Law sin? May it never be! On the contrary, I would not have come to know sin except through the Law; for I would not have known about coveting if the Law had not said, "YOU SHALL NOT COVET." But sin, taking opportunity through the commandment, produced in me coveting of every kind; for apart from the Law sin is dead.

If you don't believe that the law has this capacity, then try telling your children they can go one place but not another. The moment you say that, where do they want to go? Adam and Eve could eat from any tree in the garden except for one. It seems like the forbidden fruit is the most desirable. When I was young, I had some Catholic friends. Their parish posted a list of movies they couldn't see…which quickly became a list of movies to see. Those were the movies they wanted to see! They copied the list of forbidden movies and shared it with others.

Living in Balance

Imagine walking up a mountain road on a narrow path. To the right of the path is a cliff. It is too steep to climb down and too far down to jump. It is a tempting choice, however. You could sail off that cliff and enjoy an exhilarating "flight." You could be like the man who jumped off the top of the Empire State Building and was heard saying on the way down, "So far so good!" There are serious consequences to that choice, however, like the sudden stop at the end! Temptation entices us to live independently of God without considering the consequences. All temptations look good, or it wouldn't be tempting. Very few people are tempted to eat cooked spinach.

To the left of that road is a roaring fire. The "accuser of the brethren" has a field day with those who choose to deviate from the narrow path by reverting to the law. Many Christians are burned by legalism. Some become perfectionists, trying desperately to live up to the law. Others feel so condemned by their failures that they stay away from churches and friends who they feel may be inclined to put another guilt trip on them. Paul warned us, "It was for freedom that Christ set us free; therefore keep standing firm and do not be subject again to a yoke of slavery. Behold I, Paul, say to you that if you accept circumcision, Christ will be no advantage to you" (Galatians 5:1-2). In other words, don't go back to the law.

The devil is a tempter. He wants us to jump off that cliff. *Go on and do it. Everybody's doing it. You'll get away with it. Who would know? You know you want to.* As soon as you give in to the temptation, his role changes from tempter to accuser. *You're sick. And you call yourself a Christian. You'll never get away with this. God can't possibly love such a miserable failure as you. You deserve to burn in hell.*

So if walking by the Spirit is not license, and it's not legalism, then what is it? It is liberty: "Now the Lord is the Spirit, and where the Spirit of the Lord is, there is liberty" (2 Corinthians 3:17). How do we experience a liberated walk with God?

Walking with God

Walking by the Spirit is not passively sitting around expecting God to do it all. Nor is walking by the Spirit running around in endless, exhausting activities as though everything depended on our own efforts. Jesus said, "Apart from Me you can do nothing" (John 15:5). Paul said, "I planted, Apollos watered, but God was causing the growth" (1 Corinthians 3:6). If there is no watering or planting, nothing grows, but there is no growth without God. We are children of God, guided by His Spirit, and enabled by His presence to grow and bear fruit. There was a pastor whose favorite hobby was gardening. One day a neighbor walked by and said, "Boy, the Lord sure gave you a beautiful garden." The pastor responded, "You should have seen it when the Lord had it all by Himself."

Taking on Jesus's Yoke

Jesus said, "Come to Me, all who are weary and heavy-laden, and I will give you rest. Take My yoke upon you and learn from Me, for I am gentle and humble in heart, and you will find rest for your souls. For my yoke is easy and my burden is light" (Matthew 11:28-30). Jesus was a carpenter in His youth, but carpenters didn't frame houses as they do today. They fashioned yokes and doors, both of which Jesus would use as metaphors of Himself.

A yoke is used to harness two oxen together. When a young ox was being broken in, it was paired with a mature ox. A mature ox is like Jesus who, "although he was a son, he learned obedience through what he suffered" (Hebrews 5:8 ESV). Mature oxen have learned to walk a steady pace so as to not burn out before the day is done. They have learned not to stray off to the left or to the right. Having had much training, the lead ox already knew the best way to accomplish a day's work. He also knows that the yoke only works if the two are pulling together and going in the same direction. If there is only one in the yoke it is best not to have it on.

Young oxen get impatient with the slow pace and want to run ahead. Do you know what they get? A sore neck! Other young oxen feel like doing nothing and just want to stand still. Guess what they get? A sore neck. The lead ox is going to keep right on walking no matter what the young ox does because he is listening to his master. Whether we sit down or drop out, life goes on. The smart young ox will say, *I think I will follow the lead and learn from this old ox. He knows how to walk.* When we are yoked with Jesus, He will maintain a steady pace right down the center of the narrow path. "He gives power to the faint, and to him who has no might he increases strength. Even youths shall faint and be weary, and young men shall fall exhausted; but they who wait for the LORD shall renew their strength; they shall mount up with wings like eagles; they shall run and not be weary; they shall walk and not faint" (Isaiah 40:31 ESV).

When my children were little, we had a perfect family dog. When little Missy died, it was traumatic for all of us. I hurried to a pet store the same day and bought a replacement dog. This is a disastrous marriage-on-the-rebound story. Buster grew up to be a DAWG! He was the most neurotic mess I've ever seen. For some reason my son liked that dumb dog. So I signed up for 12 lessons at a dog obedience class, bought a choke chain, and sent my son and Buster off to be trained. Buster did a pretty good job of training my son, who gave up after two weeks.

One day I decided to give Buster a lesson in walking with his master. So I put the choke chain around his neck, and we went for a walk. I was the master, and I knew where I wanted to walk. I said walk—not run! That dumb dog nearly choked himself to death trying to run on ahead the moment we opened the door. When Buster stopped to sniff a flower or some gross thing, I kept on walking, determined to teach that dog to walk by his master. The walk became a drag. Then he would stray off the path and end up winding his leash around a tree. As I kept on walking, the result was like a wild ride at an amusement park. You ask, "Did that dumb dog ever learn to walk obediently by his master?" No, he never did. There are a few Christians who haven't either.

Jesus said, *Come to Me. I'm the lead ox. Are you weary and heavy-laden? I'll give you rest. Take My yoke upon you.* The flesh responds, *That's all I need—another yoke!* But when you put on the yoke of Christ, you throw off the yokes of legalism and license. Jesus may be a crutch, but He is the only one we need. "Learn from Me," Jesus said. What would we learn if we walked with Jesus? We would learn to take one day at a time. We would learn the priority of relationships. We would learn that our walk is one of faith, not sight, and one of grace, not legalism. We would learn to walk by faith in the power of the Holy Spirit and not succumb to outbursts of anger and other patterns of the flesh.

Jesus said, "My yoke is easy and My burden is light." If we find ourselves huffing and puffing our way through life, maybe we're not walking with God. Maybe we're running in the flesh. Matthew 11:29 is the only place in the New Testament where Jesus described Himself. He said, "I am gentle and humble in heart." We have been invited to walk with the gentle and humble Jesus. Imagine that! "Therefore as you have received Christ Jesus the Lord, so walk in Him" (Colossians 2:6).

Following Our Guide

The Holy Spirit also leads us. Being led by the Spirit is defined by two boundaries as well. First, the Holy Spirit is not pushing us. Motivated by guilt, many Christians can't seem to say *no*. They expend a lot of energy, but they bear very little fruit. They measure success in ministry by the number of activities, and spirituality by the expenditure of human energy. There is a major difference between being called into ministry and being driven to perform. The latter leads to burnout.

Second, we are not being lured away by the Holy Spirit. If you are being pressured to make a hasty decision, just say *no*—because God doesn't lead that way. The devil does. He demands an answer right now and withdraws the offer if time for consideration is requested. The guidance of God may come suddenly, but it never comes to the spiritually unprepared. Pentecost was sudden, but the disciples had spent ten days in prayerful preparation.

Believers can be lured away by various impulses. The lures of knowledge and power are ploys by Satan. We already have all the power we need in Christ (Ephesians 1:18-19). In the high priestly prayer, Jesus prayed, "I do not ask that you take them out of the world, but that you keep them from the evil one…Sanctify them in the truth; your word is truth" (John 17:15,17 ESV). The Holy Spirit will lead us into all truth.

Growing up on a farm, I had the privilege to raise championship stock sheep. I can tell you from experience that sheep are not the smartest animals on the farm. They rank right up there with chickens. For instance, you can self-feed cattle and pigs, but you can't do this with sheep. If you turn sheep loose in a green pasture without a shepherd, they will literally eat themselves to death. The Shepherd "makes me lie down in green pastures" (Psalm 23:2).

In the Western world, we drive sheep from the rear. The Australian sheepdogs and border collies bark at the heels of the sheep. However, that is not the case in Israel. When I studied at the

Institute of Holy Land Studies in Israel, I observed shepherds sitting patiently while the flock fed on the grass. When an area was sufficiently grazed, the shepherd would say something and walk off. The sheep looked up and followed him. The true shepherd doesn't chase from the back, he leads from the front. "My sheep hear My voice, and I know them, and they follow Me" (John 10:27).

Walking by the Spirit is neither legalism nor license. It's not sitting passively, waiting for God to do something, nor is it running around in endless activities trying to accomplish something by our own strength and resources. If we walk by the Spirit, we are neither driven nor lured off the path of faith, "for all who are being led by the Spirit of God, these are sons of God" (Romans 8:14). Join us in prayer:

> *Dear Heavenly Father,*
>
> *You are a righteous judge, and a God who feels indignation every day toward evil in this world (Psalm 7:11). You have warned us that there will be a great day of judgment when Your wrath will come upon the unrepentant (Revelation 6:17). Thankfully You are also slow to anger and abounding in love (Psalm 145:8). It was because of Your great love that You chose to save all who believe by sending Jesus to atone for all our sins. For our sake You made Him to be sin who knew no sin, so that in Him I become the righteousness of God (2 Corinthians 5:21). Jesus took upon Himself my sin in order that I would be saved from the wrath that is to come. I was a child of wrath (Ephesians 2:3). Now I am a child of God because of Your great love. I didn't deserve Your forgiveness, and I didn't earn Your love. I thank and praise You for Your grace and mercy.*
>
> *Lord, I have struggled with my anger and lost my patience many times. I have been self-centered and not always done unto others as I would have them do unto me. I have thought too highly of myself, and not enough about*

the needs of others. I have cried out for justice when I should have shown mercy and grace. I have been proud when I should have shown humility. I have rebelled when I should have submitted to governing authorities. I have been bitter toward others when I should have forgiven them.

I don't want to live that way anymore. I want to be like You. To be merciful as You have been merciful to me. To give unto others as You have given to me. To forgive others as You have forgiven me. Please fill me with Your Holy Spirit, and teach me how to be angry and not sin. Enable my righteous anger to become righteous deeds. I ask that You convict me of unrighteous anger and don't permit me to let the sun go down on my wrath. Keep me from letting the devil gain any foothold in my life because of my unrepentance. Thank You for healing my wounds and forgiving my sins.

I choose to put away all bitterness, wrath, anger, clamor, slander, and all malice. I choose instead to be kind, tenderhearted, and forgiving. I accept Your forgiveness, and I receive Your love. May it flow through me to others. I ask You to complete Your good work in me that began the day I became Your child. I yield my body to You as a living sacrifice and seek to be transformed by the renewing of my mind, believing that Your will is good, acceptable, and perfect.

I love You, Lord, and I pray all this in Your wonderful name. Amen.

Discussion Questions

1. Why must we have a balanced understanding of who God is?

2. Who is angrier? The liberal or the legalist?

3. Does a legalist know he or she is a legalist?

4. How is relating to God under the New Covenant different from relating to God under the Old Covenant?

5. What is the difference between license and freedom?

6. What are the three biblical reasons why legalism doesn't work?

7. How does the devil get us off the narrow path?

8. How can we find the balance between sitting, walking, and running with Jesus?

9. What is the value of taking on Jesus's yoke?

10. What is the difference between being led by Jesus and being lured or pushed by Satan?

Go in peace.

GUIDELINES FOR LEADING THIS STUDY OF *MANAGING YOUR ANGER*

The normal guidelines for leading a group study apply to this book as well:

1. Encourage participants to come prepared by reading each chapter before the meeting.

2. Create an atmosphere of trust by using the first meeting to get acquainted. Spend some time getting to know one another. Share prayer requests, and encourage the group to pray for one another.

3. As best as you can, ensure confidentiality.

4. Encourage safe self-disclosure without judgment, but don't permit gossip about others.

5. State at the beginning that everyone's participation is desired, but it is your responsibility as the leader to ensure that no one person dominates the discussion, and that includes you.

6. There are no foolish questions.

7. Everyone's opinion is to be respected.

After you have completed the discussion questions, finish by leading them through one of the *Steps to Freedom in Christ* (Steps). Each of chapters 2-8 include a step. The first chapter includes an introduction to the Steps, so be sure to take the time to read this introduction in your group. The gospel is also explained and followed by a prayer for salvation. If you feel it is appropriate, have the group pray the prayer out loud together. If they are all believers they will not a have a problem with that. There is also a prayer and declaration that begins the Steps. Have them pray and make the declaration together out loud.

Each Step begins with a prayer asking God to guide them. These prayers should be read out loud together. After this, give participants several minutes to finish the Step on their own. This is an encounter between themselves and God. They can do it or not do it. It is up to them. Be sure to tell everyone that nobody will be embarrassed and nobody will be asked to share personal and intimate details of their lives. If anyone is having difficulty with the Steps, talk to them privately. The Steps are not complete until the final Step in chapter 8.

NOTES

Introduction

1. John Marks, "The American Uncivil Wars," *U.S. News Online*, April 22, 1996, 2.
2. Mark Galli, "Beautiful Orthodox," *Christianity Today*, October, 2016, 36.
3. *Esquire* editors, *American Rage: The Esquire/NBC News Survey*, January 3, 2016.

Chapter 1

1. "Boiling Point" presented at the Mental Health Action Week, 2008, Mental Health Organization.
2. S.I. McMillen, MD, *None of These Diseases* (Minneapolis, MN: Successful Living, Inc., 1963), 69.
3. Frederick Buechner, *Wishful Thinking: A Theological ABC* (New York: Harper & Row, 1973), 2.
4. Meyer Friedman and Ray Rosenman, *Type A Behavior and Your Heart* (New York: Knopf, 1974).
5. Redford and Virginia Williams, *Anger Kills* (New York: Harper Perennial, 1993).
6. Ibid., 60.
7. Some theologians prefer the dichotomist perspective and understand that the human soul and spirit are essentially the same. Others prefer the trichotomist perspective and understand that the human soul and spirit are distinct from each other. Neither perspective is in conflict with what we are presenting.

Chapter 2

1. George Sweeting, *Great Quotes & Illustrations* (Waco, TX: Word Books, 1985), 16.
2. The Greek word *noema* is here translated as "thought." It occurs three other places in 2 Corinthians. In 2:10-11 (ESV) we are urged to forgive, "so that we would not be outwitted by Satan; for we are not ignorant of his *designs* [*noema*]." In 4:3-4 (ESV), "If our gospel is veiled, it is veiled only to those who are perishing. In their case the god of this world [Satan] has blinded the minds [*noema*] of the unbelievers." In 10:5 (ESV), "We destroy arguments and every lofty opinion raised against the knowledge of God, and take every thought [*noema*] captive to obey Christ." We cannot overlook the spiritual connection to that word.

3. The Board of the Ministry of Healing is chaired by Dr. George Hurst, who previously directed the University of Texas Health Center at Tyler, Texas, george.hurst@uthct.edu. The Oklahoma and Texas data were combined together in a manuscript that was accepted by the *Southern Medical Journal* for publication (Volume 101, Issue 4, April 2008).

4. J.R. Averill, "Studies of Anger and Aggression: Implications for Theories of Emotion," *American Psychologist* 38 (1983), 1145-60.

5. W. Doyle Gentry, PhD, *Anger Free* (New York: Quill, 1999), 114.

6. Neil T. Anderson, *Discipleship Counseling* (Minneapolis, MN: Bethany House, 2003).

7. Leon Morris, *The First Epistle of Paul to the Corinthians*, Tyndale New Testament Commentary (Grand Rapids, MI: Wm. B. Eerdmans, 1976), 75.

8. Robert D. Sherer, *Fear, the Corporate F Word: How to Drive Out the Fear That Kills Productivity and Profits* (self-published, 1996).

9. From the poem "Disappointment—His Appointment," by Edith Lillian Young, date and publisher unknown.

Chapter 3

1. D.L. Thomas and A.J. Weigert, "Socialization and Adolescent Conformity to Significant Others: A Cross-National Analysis," *American Sociological Review*, vol. 36 (October, 1971), adapted from pages 835-47.

2. Gary Chapman, *The Other Side of Love* (Chicago, IL: Moody Press, 1999), 18-19.

3. Bob Benson, *Laughter in the Walls* (Nashville, TN: Impact Books, 1969), 68.

Chapter 4

1. Carnality is our fallen human nature derived from living independently from God. The carnal person is governed by human nature instead of by the Spirit of God. *Carnal* is often translated as "fleshly" or "of the flesh."

Chapter 5

1. Neil Anderson and Mike and Julia Quarles, *Freedom from Addiction* (Ventura, CA: Regal Books, 1996), 40.

Chapter 6

1. William R. Moody, *The Life of Dwight L. Moody* (Murfreesboro, TN: Sword of the Lord Publishers, n.d.), 110-11.

2. Ron and Pat Potter-Efron, *Letting Go of Anger* (Oakland, CA: New Harbinger Publications, Inc., 1995), 6.

3. Ken Voges and Ron Braund, *Understanding How Others Misunderstand You* (Chicago, IL: Moody Press, 1990), 38-41.

4. Ibid., 71.

5. Potter-Efron, *Letting Go of Anger*, 104.

6. Les Carter and Frank Minirth, *The Anger Workbook* (Nashville, TN: Thomas Nelson, 1992), 32.

Chapter 7

1. Robert J. Morgan, *Stories, Illustrations & Quotes* (Nashville, TN: Thomas Nelson, 2000), 71-72.

2. Source unknown.

Chapter 8

1. S.J. De Vries, "Sin, sinners," eds. G. Buttrick et al, *The Interpreter's Dictionary of the Bible* (Nashville, TN: Abingdon, 1962), 365.

2. Francis Brown, S. Drive, and Charles Briggs, *Hebrew and English Lexicon* (Peabody, MA: Hendrickson, 1996), n.p.

3. Neil T. Anderson, *Becoming a Disciple-Making Church* (Minneapolis, MN: Bethany House, 2016), 52-54.

Chapter 9

1. Neil T. Anderson, Rich Miller, and Paul Travis, *Grace That Breaks the Chains* (Eugene, OR: Harvest House Publishers, 2003).

DR. NEIL T. ANDERSON
AND RICH MILLER

Core Material

Victory Over the Darkness offers a study guide, audiobook, and DVD (Bethany House, 2000). With over 1,400,000 copies in print, this core book explains who you are in Christ, how to walk by faith in the power of the Holy Spirit, how to be transformed by the renewing of your mind, how to experience emotional freedom, and how to relate to one another in Christ.

The Bondage Breaker offers a study guide and audiobook (Harvest House Publishers, 2000). With over 1,400,000 copies in print, this book explains spiritual warfare, what our protection is, ways that we are vulnerable, and how we can live a liberated life in Christ

Discipleship Counseling (Bethany House, 2003) combines the concepts of discipleship and counseling and teaches the practical integration of theology and psychology for helping Christians resolve their personal and spiritual conflicts through repentance and faith in God.

Steps to Freedom in Christ and interactive DVD (Bethany House, 2017) is a discipleship counseling tool that helps Christians resolve their personal and spiritual conflicts through genuine repentance and faith in God.

Restored (E3 Resources) is an expansion of the *Steps to Freedom in Christ* with additional explanation and instruction.

Walking in Freedom (Bethany House, 2008) is a 21-day devotional used for follow-up after leading someone through the Steps to Freedom.

Freedom in Christ (Bethany House, 2008) is a discipleship course for Sunday school classes and small groups. The course comes with a teacher's guide, a student guide and a DVD covering 12 lessons and the *Steps to Freedom in Christ*. This course is designed to enable believers to resolve personal and spiritual conflicts and be established alive and free in Christ.

The Bondage Breaker DVD Experience (Harvest House, 2011) is also a discipleship course for Sunday school classes and small groups. It is similar to the one above, but the lessons are 15 minutes instead of 30 minutes. It offers a student guide, but no teacher's guide.

Victory Series (Bethany House, 2014, 2015) is a comprehensive curriculum, including eight books that follow the growth sequence of being rooted in Christ, growing in Christ, living in Christ, and overcoming in Christ: *God's Story for You, Your New Identity, Your Foundation in Christ, Renewing Your Mind, Growing in Christ, Your Life in Christ, Your Authority in Christ, Your Ultimate Victory*.

Specialized Books

The Bondage Breaker, The Next Step (Harvest House, 2011) has several testimonies of people who found their freedom from all kinds of problems with commentary by Dr. Anderson. It is an important learning tool for encouragers and gives hope to those who are entangled in sin.

Overcoming Addictive Behavior with Mike Quarles (Bethany House, 2003) explores the path to addiction and how a Christian can overcome addictive behaviors.

Overcoming Depression with Joanne Anderson (Bethany House, 2004) explores the nature of depression, which is a body, soul, and spirit problem and presents a "wholistic" answer for overcoming this "common cold" of mental illnesses.

Daily in Christ with Joanne Anderson (Harvest House Publishers, 2000) is a popular daily devotional read by thousands of Internet subscribers every day.

Who I Am in Christ (Bethany House, 2001) has 36 short chapters describing who believers are in Christ and how their deepest needs are met in Him.

Freedom from Addiction with Mike and Julia Quarles (Bethany House, 1997) begins with Mike and Julia's journey into addiction and co-dependency and explains the nature of chemical addictions and how to overcome them in Christ.

One Day at a Time with Mike Quarles (Bethany House, 2000) is a 365-day devotional helping those who struggle with addictive behaviors and explains how to discover the grace of God on a daily basis.

Freedom from Fear with Rich Miller (Harvest House Publishers, 1999) explains the nature of fear, anxiety, and panic attacks and how to overcome them.

Setting Your Church Free with Dr. Charles Mylander (Bethany House, 2006, 2014) explains servant leadership and how the leadership of a church can resolve corporate conflicts through corporate repentance.

Setting Your Marriage Free with Dr. Charles Mylander (Bethany House, 2006, 2014) explains God's divine plan for marriage and the steps that couples can take to resolve their difficulties.

Christ-Centered Therapy with Dr. Terry and Julie Zuehlke (Zondervan Publishing House, 2000) explains the practical integration of theology and psychology for professional counselors and provides them with biblical tools for therapy.

Put Away All Anger with Rich Miller (Harvest House Publishers, 1999) explains the basis for anger and how to put away all anger, wrath, and malice.

Grace That Breaks the Chains with Rich Miller and Paul Travis (Harvest House Publishers, 2003, 2014) explains the bondage of legalism and how to overcome it by the grace of God.

Winning the Battle Within (Harvest House, 2008) shares God's standards for sexual conduct, the path to sexual addiction, and how to overcome sexual strongholds.

Restoring Broken Relationships (Bethany House, 2008) explains the primary ministry of the church and how we can be reconciled to God and each other.

Rough Road to Freedom (Monarch Books) is Dr. Anderson's memoirs.

The Power of Presence (Monarch Books) is about experiencing the presence of God during difficult times and what our presence means to each other. This book is written in the context of Dr. Anderson caring for his wife who is slowly dying with agitated dementia.

For more information or to purchase the above materials, contact Freedom in Christ Ministries:

Canada:	freedominchrist@sasktel.net	www.ficm.ca
United Kingdom:	info@ficm.org.ukw	www.ficm.org.uk
United States:	info@ficm.org	www.ficm.org
International:	www.ficminternational.org	

To learn more about Harvest House books and
to read sample chapters, visit our website:

www.harvesthousepublishers.com

HARVEST HOUSE PUBLISHERS
EUGENE, OREGON